Treasures

A Reading/Language Arts Program

Macmillan
McGraw-Hill

Contributors

Time Magazine, Accelerated Reader

RFB&D 🎧
learning through listening

Students with print disabilities may be eligible to obtain an accessible, audio version of the pupil edition of this textbook. Please call Recording for the Blind & Dyslexic at 1-800-221-4792 for complete information.

B

The McGraw·Hill Companies

Macmillan McGraw-Hill

Published by Macmillan/McGraw-Hill, of McGraw-Hill Education, a division of The McGraw-Hill Companies, Inc., Two Penn Plaza, New York, New York 10121.

Printed in the United States of America

ISBN 0-02-192008-7/3, Bk. 1

5 6 7 8 9 (058/043) 09 08 07

Treasures

A Reading/Language Arts Program

Program Authors

Donald R. Bear
Janice A. Dole
Jana Echevarria
Jan E. Hasbrouck
Scott G. Paris
Timothy Shanahan
Josefina V. Tinajero

Macmillan
McGraw-Hill

THEME: New Beginnings

Talk About It 10

Tina's Try-Out Day
Vocabulary/Comprehension: Character, Setting, Plot . . . 12

First Day Jitters Humorous Fiction 14
By Julie Danneberg, illustrated by Judy Love

Making New Friends Health 34
By Jan Smith

Writing: **Personal Narrative** 36

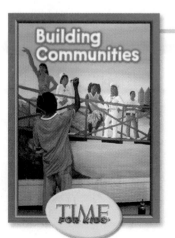

THEME: Keeping in Touch

Talk About It 38

Mail for Matty
Vocabulary/Comprehension: Character, Setting, Plot . . 40

Dear Juno Realistic Fiction 42
By Soyung Pak, illustrated by Susan Kathleen Hartung

How We Keep in Touch Social Studies 68
By Eric Michaels

Writing: **Personal Narrative** 72

THEME: Building Communities

Talk About It 74

Home Sweet Harlem
Vocabulary/Comprehension: Main Idea and Details 76

Whose Habitat Is It? Nonfiction Article 78

All Are Equal: It's the Law! Social Studies . . 82

Writing: **Extended Response to Literature** 84

THEME: Antarctic Life

Talk About It 86

Life in Antarctica
    Vocabulary/Comprehension: Main Idea and Details 88

Penguin Chick (Narrative Nonfiction) 90
    By Betty Tatham, illustrated by Helen K. Davie

Antarctic Anthem (Poetry) 112
    By Judy Sierra

Writing: **Poem** 114

THEME: People and Their Pets

Talk About It 116

Choosing a Pet
    Vocabulary/Comprehension: Problem and Solution 118

The Perfect Pet (Humorous Fiction) 120
    By Margie Palatini, illustrated by Bruce Whatley

Pets: True or False? (Science) 142
    By Gillian Reed

Writing: **Personal Narrative** 146

Test Strategy: Think and Search

Evan's Welcome (Drama) 148

Unit 2 Investigations

THEME: Putting on a Performance

Talk About It 152

The Wind and the Sun: An Aesop's Fable
Vocabulary/Comprehension: Summarize 154

The Strongest One Play .156
By Joseph Bruchac, illustrated by Lucia Angela Perez

Behind the Scenes at a Play Performing Arts 172
By Candice Bertoline

Writing: **Persuasive Writing** 176

THEME: Wolves

Talk About It 178

The Boy Who Cried Wolf
Vocabulary/Comprehension: Fantasy and Reality 180

Wolf! Fantasy 182
By Becky Bloom, illustrated by Pascal Biet

The Truth About Wolves Science 206
By Paul Netcher

Writing: **Persuasive Writing** 210

THEME: Past, Present, and Future

Talk About It 212

Where Did the First Americans Live?
Vocabulary/Comprehension: Fact and Opinion. 214

What's in Store for the Future? Nonfiction Article 216

Will Robots Do All the Work? Social Studies 220

Writing: **Personal Narrative**. 222

6

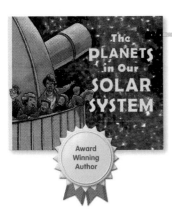

THEME: Out in Space

Talk About It 224

Constellations: Pictures in the Sky
  Vocabulary/Comprehension: Summarize 226

The Planets in Our Solar System (Informational Nonfiction) 228
  By Franklyn M. Branley, illustrated by Kevin O'Malley

Star Research (Science) 250

Writing: **Persuasive Writing** 254

THEME: Being a Writer

Talk About It 256

Talking to Lulu Delacre, Children's Author
  Vocabulary/Comprehension: Author's Purpose 258

Author: A True Story (Autobiography) 260
  By Helen Lester

Where I Sit Writing (Poetry) 274
  By Allan Ahlberg

Writing: **Persuasive Writing** 276

Test Strategy: Author and Me

Venus Flytrap: The Plant with Bite! (Informational Nonfiction) 278

Unit 3 Discoveries

THEME: Food Around the World

Talk About It 282

Family Feast
   Vocabulary/Comprehension: Make Inferences 284

Stone Soup Folktale 286
   By Jon J Muth

What's for Lunch? Social Studies 308
   By Leonard Mercury

Writing: **Personal Narrative** 312

THEME: Solving Riddles

Talk About It 314

Count on Detective Drake!
   Vocabulary/Comprehension: Plot and Setting 316

One Riddle, One Answer Fairy Tale 318
   By Lauren Thompson, illustrated by Linda S. Wingerter

Haiku Poetry 336

Writing: **Story** 338

THEME: Ecosystems in Balance

Talk About It 340

For the Birds!
   Vocabulary/Comprehension: Cause and Effect 342

Saving the Sand Dunes Nonfiction Article 344

   Frog Frenzy! Science 348

   Writing: **Persuasive Writing** 350

THEME: Making Journeys

Talk About It 352

My Winter Vacation
    Vocabulary/Comprehension: Make Inferences 354

The Jones Family Express Realistic Fiction . . 356
    By Javaka Steptoe

Tips for Trips Social Studies 380
    By Lauren Eckler

Writing: **Story** 382

THEME: The Art of Illustrating

Talk About It 384

Draw!
    Vocabulary/Comprehension: Sequence 386

**What Do
Illustrators Do?** Narrative Nonfiction 388
    By Eileen Christelow

Jobs in Animation Fine Arts 412
    By Lisa Soo

Writing: **Play** 416

Test Strategy: Right There

Design Your Own Journal Directions 418

Glossary 422

NEW BEGINNINGS

Talk About It

Change can be difficult.
How do you feel about new
people, places, and things?

LOG ON Find out more about
new beginnings at
www.macmillanmh.com

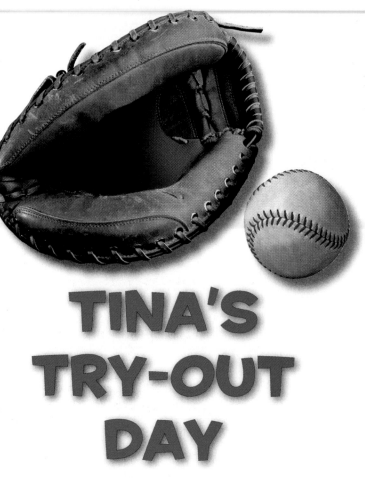

TINA'S TRY-OUT DAY

by Amy Helfer

Tina woke up to her buzzing alarm clock. She rubbed her eyes and wondered why she was up so early. Then she remembered: it was try-out day!

THE BIG DAY

A few weeks ago, Tina decided she would try out for the Comets, her school's softball team. Tina ran **downstairs** to the kitchen. "Mom!" she shouted. "It's try-out day!"

"I know," answered Mom. "I made you breakfast."

Tina rubbed her stomach. "I think I'm too **nervous** to eat."

"You'll have more energy if you do," said Mom.

Tina still felt a bit sick, but she ate some breakfast anyway. Then she ran up to her room and **fumbled** into her clothes.

"Slow down!" Mom **chuckled**. "You'll use up all your energy before you get there."

ON THE FIELD

Tina got to the field early, but it seemed like everyone else did, too.

"What am I doing here?" Tina asked herself. "I'll never make the team."

Her mom gave her a hug. "That's **nonsense,**" she said. "Get out there and do your best. You will be great!"

PLAY BALL!

The girls had to run, field, bat, catch, and throw balls. Even though Tina stumbled while fielding, she thought she did well.

Afterward, Tina was really tired and **trudged** off the field. One of the coaches called her name. "What do you think, Tina?" she asked. "Would you like to join the Comets?"

Tina forgot how tired she was and jumped high into the air. "Oh, boy," she shouted. "Would I ever!"

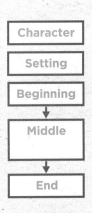

Reread for **Comprehension**

STRATEGY SKILL

Analyze Story Structure
Character, Setting, Plot

Every story has characters, a setting, and a plot. They make up the story's structure. Characters are people in the story. The setting is when and where the story takes place. The plot tells all the events in the story. It has a beginning, middle, and end.

A Story Map helps you analyze the story structure. Reread the story to find the characters, setting, and what happened at the beginning, middle, and end.

| Character |
| Setting |
| Beginning |
| ↓ |
| Middle |
| ↓ |
| End |

Comprehension

Genre

Humorous Fiction is a made-up story written to make the reader laugh.

Analyze Story Structure

Character, Setting, Plot

As you read, use your Story Map.

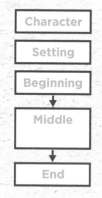

```
Character

Setting

Beginning
   ↓
Middle
   ↓
End
```

Read to Find Out

Why does Sarah try to avoid going to school?

14

FIRST DAY JITTERS

by JULIE DANNEBERG

illustrated by JUDY LOVE

Award Winning Selection

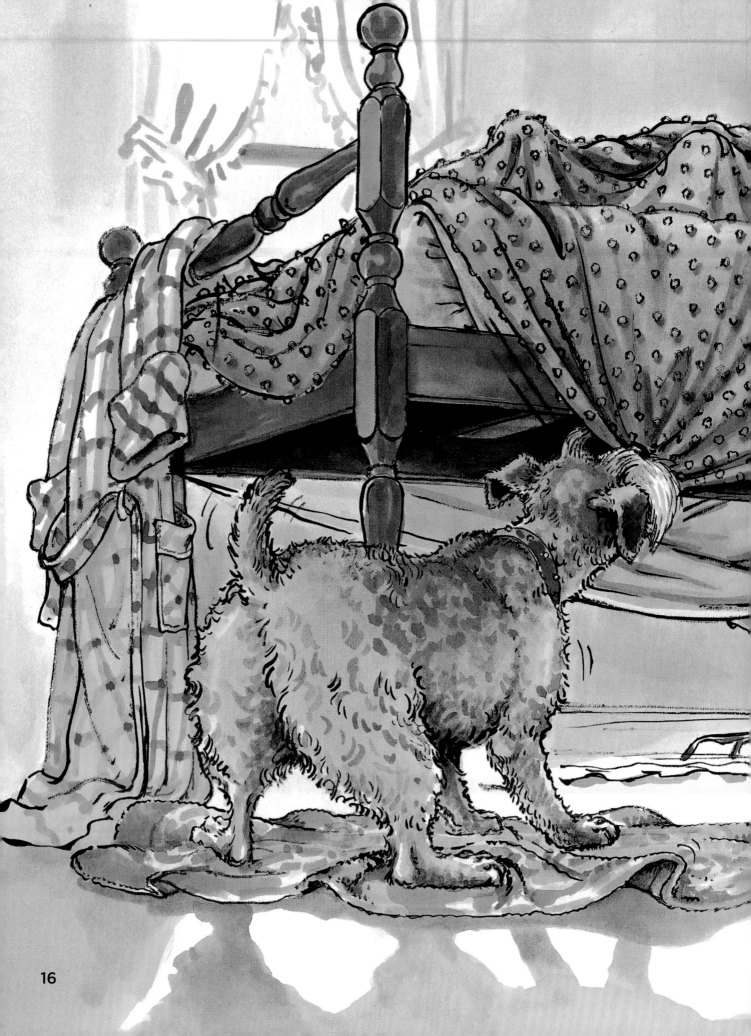

"Sarah, dear, time to get out of bed," Mr. Hartwell said, poking his head through the bedroom doorway. "You don't want to miss the first day at your new school do you?"

"I'm not going," said Sarah, and pulled the covers over her head.

"Of course you're going, honey," said Mr. Hartwell, as he walked over to the window and snapped up the shade.

"No, I'm not. I don't want to start over again. I hate my new school," Sarah said.

She tunneled down to the end of her bed.

Plot
What events have taken place so far?

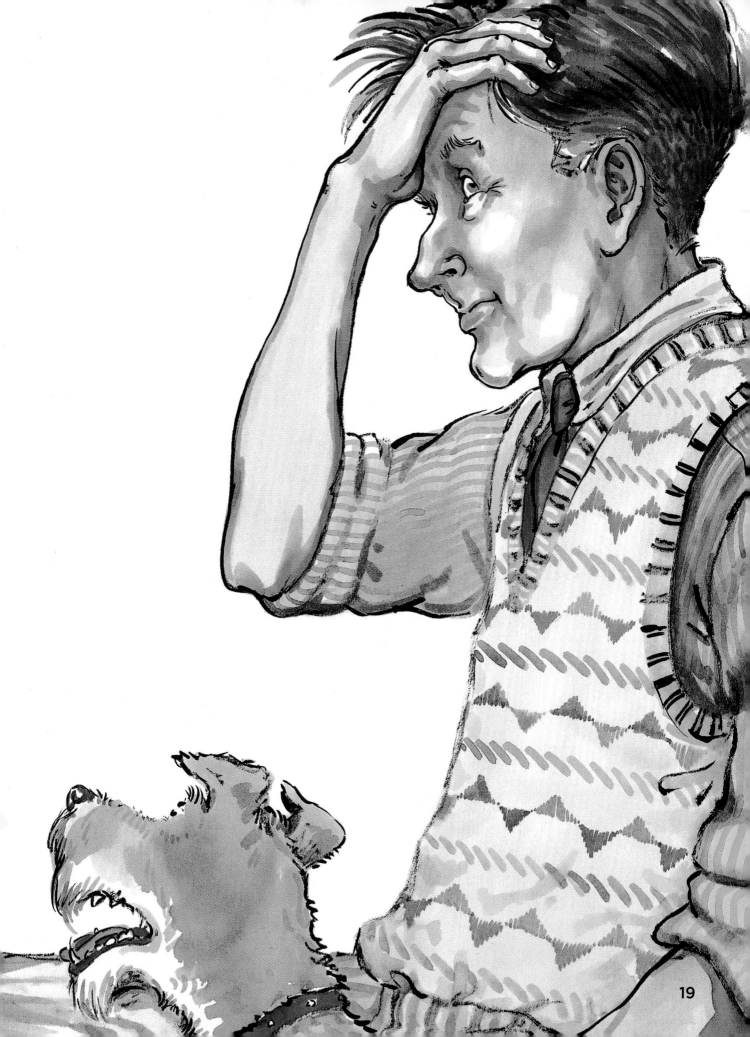

"How can you hate your new school, sweetheart?" Mr. Hartwell **chuckled**. "You've never been there before! Don't worry. You liked your other school, you'll like this one. Besides, just think of all the new friends you'll meet."

"That's just it. I don't know anybody, and it
will be hard, and ... I just hate it, that's all."

"What will everyone think if you aren't there? We told them you were coming!"

"They will think that I am lucky and they will wish that they were at home in bed like me."

Mr. Hartwell sighed. "Sarah Jane Hartwell, I'm not playing this silly game one second longer. I'll see you **downstairs** in five minutes."

Sarah
  tumbled
    out of bed.
      She stumbled into the bathroom.
      She **fumbled** into her clothes.

"My head hurts," she moaned as she
trudged into the kitchen.

Mr. Hartwell handed Sarah a piece of toast
and her lunchbox.

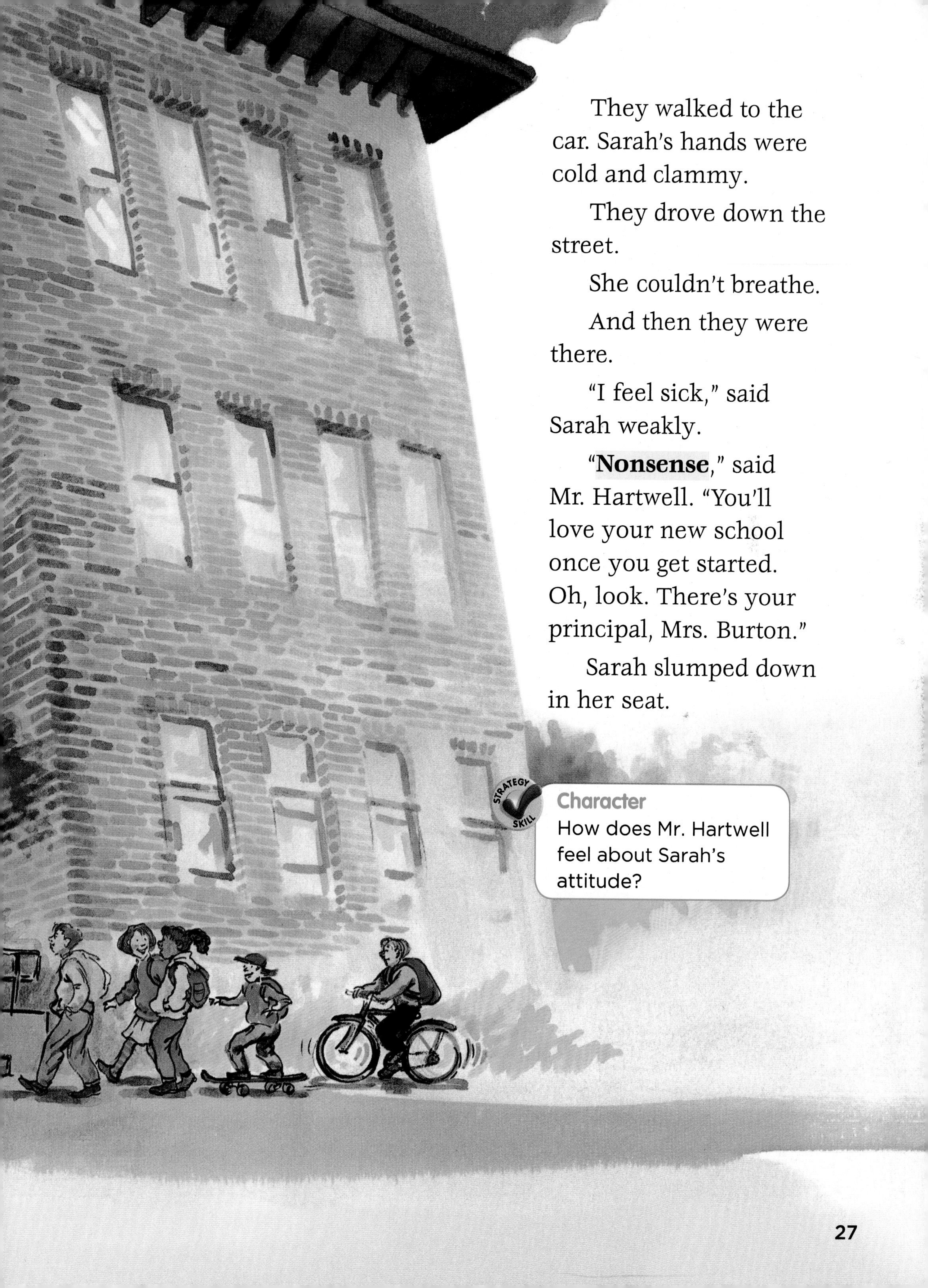

They walked to the car. Sarah's hands were cold and clammy.

They drove down the street.

She couldn't breathe.

And then they were there.

"I feel sick," said Sarah weakly.

"**Nonsense**," said Mr. Hartwell. "You'll love your new school once you get started. Oh, look. There's your principal, Mrs. Burton."

Sarah slumped down in her seat.

STRATEGY SKILL

Character
How does Mr. Hartwell feel about Sarah's attitude?

"Oh, Sarah," Mrs. Burton gushed, peeking into the car. "There you are. Come on. I'll show you where to go."

She led Sarah into the building and walked quickly through the crowded hallways. "Don't worry. Everyone is **nervous** the first day," she said over her shoulder as Sarah rushed to keep up.

When they got to the classroom, most of the children were already in their seats.

The class looked up as Mrs. Burton cleared her throat.

"Class. Class. Attention, please," said Mrs. Burton.

When the class was quiet she led Sarah to the front of the room and said, "Class, I would like you to meet …

... your new teacher, Mrs. Sarah Jane Hartwell."

OFF TO SCHOOL WITH
JULIE AND JUDY

AUTHOR

JULIE DANNEBERG knows all about teaching. She has been a teacher for many years and really enjoys it. Julie says that being around kids all day gives her lots of ideas for stories. She starts every day by working on her writing for an hour.

Another book by Julie Danneberg: *First Year Letters*

ILLUSTRATOR

JUDY LOVE decided that she wanted to illustrate books when she was seven or eight years old. Judy gets ideas for her illustrations from her favorite hobbies: gardening, visiting museums, and making costumes for children's plays.

LOG ON Find out more about Julie Danneberg and Judy Love at **www.macmillanmh.com**

Write About It

In this story, the teacher is worried about her first day of school. Describe how you felt about your first day of school as a third grader.

Comprehension Check

Retell the Story

Use your Story Map to help you retell *First Day Jitters*. Tell about what happens in the beginning, middle, and end of the story.

| Character |
| Setting |
| Beginning |
| ↓ |
| Middle |
| ↓ |
| End |

Think and Compare

1. Why was Sarah so **nervous** about going to school? **Analyze Story Structure: Plot, Character, Setting**

2. At the beginning of the story, why might most readers think Sarah was a child? Give details from the story in your answer. **Analyze**

3. How would you feel if you were a teacher on the first day at a new school? Explain. **Apply**

4. Do you think that most people are nervous about facing new, unknown situations? Explain your answer. **Evaluate**

5. Read "Tina's Try-Out Day" on pages 12–13. How is Tina's situation similar to Sarah's? How do Tina and Sarah react differently to their situations? Use details from both selections in your answer. **Reading/Writing Across Texts**

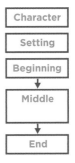

Making New Friends

by Jan Smith

It's tough being the new kid in a crowd. You want to be **accepted**. You want to be liked. What can you do to make friends? Be friendly! Here's how.

Relax and Smile

A smile **attracts** other people. When you look and feel comfortable, people will want to get to know you better.

Introduce Yourself

Don't be afraid to **introduce** yourself to people you would like to meet. They may want to meet you, too!

Ask Questions and Listen

Ask questions to find out people's interests. Listen carefully as they answer you. That shows that you're interested in getting to know them.

Find Things in Common

Maybe you like the same sports team or the same books. When it comes to making friends, you should always follow the easiest rule: Have fun! You may make some new friends before you know it.

How to Make New Friends

Reading a Bar Graph

This bar graph shows the answers to a **survey**. A survey asks what people think about something.

Survey Question: What is the most important thing to do to make new friends?

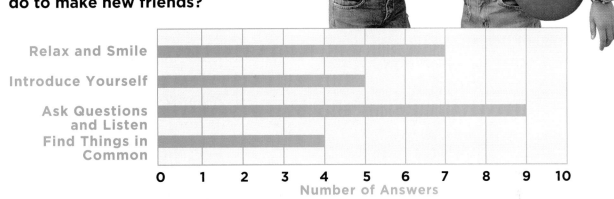

- Relax and Smile: 7
- Introduce Yourself: 5
- Ask Questions and Listen: 9
- Find Things in Common: 4

Number of Answers (0–10)

Connect and Compare

1. Look at the bar graph. How many people answered that the most important thing to do is to ask questions and listen? How do you know? **Reading a Bar Graph**

2. The next time you are around new people, what will you do to make friends? Explain your answer. **Apply**

3. Sarah was nervous about meeting new students. After reading "Making New Friends," what advice could you give Sarah about getting to know her students? **Reading/Writing Across Texts**

 Health Activity

With a partner, brainstorm four things you like to do with your friends. Survey your classmates and make a bar graph to compare their answers.

LOG ON Find out more about making friends at **www.macmillanmh.com**

Writing

Organization

The topic sentence is at the start of the paragraph. It tells the reader the main idea of the paragraph. The other sentences give supporting details.

★ Write About ★ the First Day ★ of School ★

I wanted to tell about my first day in the third grade. This is what I wrote.

First, I wrote a topic sentence. Then, I wrote sentences with supporting details.

Wrong Room!

by Ricardo Z.

My first day of third grade didn't start well. First, my mom had to go to work early. She left right after rushing me to my classroom. I waited inside for a while before the other kids started coming. They looked huge. I never saw them before in my life. I was scared. Where was my friend Harry? Where was Jen? We were supposed to be in the same class. Then the teacher said, "Hello, Class 5-B." I was so happy. I was supposed to be in class 3-B. I was just sitting in the wrong room!

Your Turn

Write a paragraph about an experience you had on the first day of school. It may be about meeting a new friend or about something that happened. Be sure to begin your paragraph with a topic sentence that tells the main idea. Then include supporting details in the sentences that follow. Use the Writer's Checklist to check your writing.

Writer's Checklist

☑ **Ideas and Content:** Are my story details interesting?

☐ **Organization:** Does my story have a topic sentence and supporting details?

☑ **Voice:** Does the writing sound like me?

☑ **Word Choice:** Did I choose words that clearly tell how I felt?

☑ **Sentence Fluency:** Did I write in complete sentences?

☑ **Conventions:** Did I start sentences with capital letters? Did I spell and use end punctuation correctly?

KEEPING
IN
TOUCH

Talk About It

How do you keep in touch with family and friends who are far away?

LOG ON Find out more about keeping in touch at **www.macmillanmh.com**

Mail for Matty

by Susan Tanner

Nana has been visiting for two weeks, but now it's time for her to go home. I wish she could stay.

At the Airport

"Why so sad, Matty? I'm going home, not to the moon!" joked Nana.

"Montana's so far away, it might as well be the moon," I answered. I tightened my hold on Nana's plane ticket until it began to **crackle**.

Nana laughed. "Oh, it's not that far! You'll see me soon," she said. "I promise."

Just then a voice on the loudspeaker **announced** that Nana's flight was boarding.

"Time to go," said Nana. "When I get home, I'll send you a surprise. Watch for it!" She hugged us good-bye. We waited until her plane **soared** up high into the dark but **starry** sky. I wondered what my surprise was.

Waiting for the Surprise

When I got home, I kept checking the door and looking out the window for my surprise. Then Dad called, "Hey, Matty, come over here!"

Dad was at the computer. The screen showed a picture of an **envelope**. I had e-mail! The title of the e-mail said "Surprise!" It read:

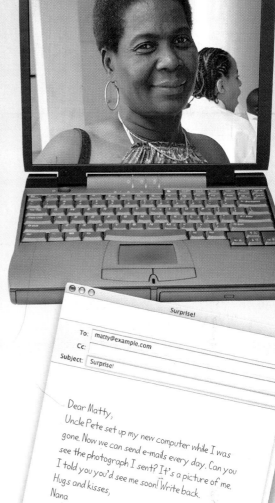

Dear Matty,

Uncle Pete set up my new computer while I was gone. Now we can send e-mails every day. Can you see the **photograph** I sent? It's a picture of me. I told you you'd see me soon! Write back.

Hugs and kisses,

Nana

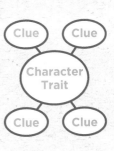

Surprise!

To: matty@example.com
Cc:
Subject: Surprise!

Dear Matty,
Uncle Pete set up my new computer while I was gone. Now we can send e-mails every day. Can you see the photograph I sent? It's a picture of me. I told you you'd see me soon! Write back.
Hugs and kisses,
Nana

Nana did surprise me! I'm so excited that I can talk to her every day.

Reread for **Comprehension**

Analyze Story Structure

Character, Setting, Plot

Every story has characters, a setting, and a plot. These elements make up the story's structure. The main character is the person who the story is about.

A Character Web helps you figure out a character's traits, or personality. Reread "Mail for Matty." What one thing can you tell about Matty's character based on what he does and thinks after Nana leaves?

Clue Clue
Character Trait
Clue Clue

Comprehension

Genre

Realistic Fiction is an invented story that could have happened in real life.

Analyze Story Structure

Character, Setting, Plot
As you read, use your Character web.

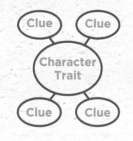

Read to Find Out

How does Juno try to communicate with his grandmother?

Dear Juno

by Soyung Pak

illustrated by

Susan Kathleen Hartung

Award Winning
Author
and
Illustrator

Juno watched as the red and white blinking lights **soared** across the night sky like shooting stars, and waited as they disappeared into faraway places. Juno wondered where they came from. He wondered where they were going. And he wondered if any of the planes came from a little town near Seoul where his grandmother lived, and where she ate persimmons every evening before bed.

Juno looked at the letter that came that day. It was long and white and smudged. He saw the red and blue marks on the edges and knew the letter came from far away. His name and address were neatly printed on the front, so he knew the letter was for him. But best of all, the special stamp on the corner told Juno that the letter was from his grandmother.

STRATEGY SKILL

Character
What do Juno's thoughts and actions tell you about him?

Through the window Juno could see his parents. He
saw bubbles growing in the sink. He saw dirty dishes
waiting to be washed. He knew he would have to wait
for the cleaning to be done before his parents could
read the letter to him.

"Maybe I can read the inside, too," Juno said to his dog, Sam. Sam wagged his tail. Very carefully, Juno opened the **envelope**. Inside, he found a letter folded into a neat, small square.

He unfolded it. Tucked inside were a picture and a dried flower.

Juno looked at the letters and words he couldn't understand. He pulled out the **photograph**. It was a picture of his grandmother holding a cat. He pulled out the red and yellow flower. It felt light and gentle like a dried leaf. Juno smiled. "C'mon, Sam," Juno said. "Let's find Mom and Dad."

49

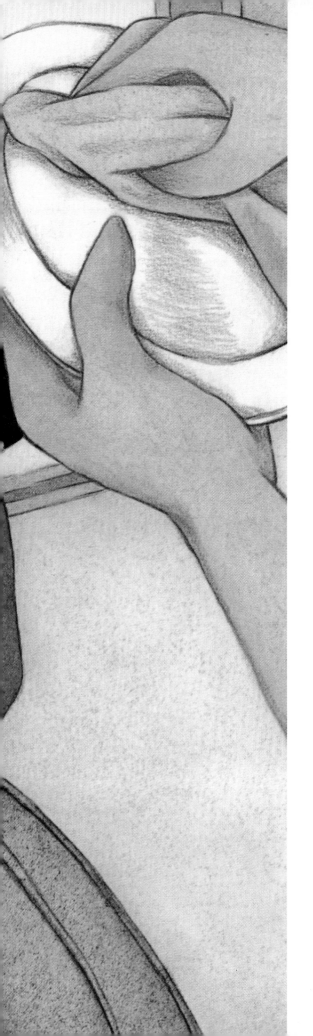

"Grandma has a new cat," Juno said as he handed the letter to his mother. "And she's growing red and yellow flowers in her garden."

"How do you know she has a new cat?" Juno's father asked.

"She wouldn't send me a picture of a strange cat," said Juno.

"I guess not," said Juno's father.

"How do you know the flower is from her garden?" asked Juno's mother.

"She wouldn't send me a flower from someone else's garden," Juno answered.

"No, she wouldn't," said Juno's mother.

Then Juno's mother read him the letter.

Character
How can you tell Juno is smart?

Dear Juno,

How are you? I have a new cat to keep me company. I named him Juno after you. He can't help me weed, but the rabbits no longer come to eat my flowers.

Grandma

"Just like you read it yourself," Juno's father said.

"I did read it," Juno said.

"Yes, you did," said his mother.

First, he drew a picture of his mom and dad standing outside the house. Second, he drew a picture of Sam playing underneath his big swinging tree. Then very carefully, Juno drew a picture of himself standing under an airplane in a **starry**, nighttime sky. After he was finished, he placed everything in the envelope.

"Here's my letter," Juno **announced** proudly. "You can read it if you want."

Juno's father looked in the envelope.

He pulled out the leaf. "Only a big swinging tree could grow a leaf this big," he said.

Juno's mother pulled out one of the drawings. "What a fine picture," she said. "It takes a good artist to say so much with a drawing."

Juno's father patted Juno on the head. "It's just like a real letter," he said.

"It is a real letter," Juno said.

"It certainly is," said his mother. Then they mailed the envelope and waited.

One day a big envelope came. It was from Juno's grandmother. This time, Juno didn't wait at all. He opened the envelope right away.

Inside, Juno found a box of colored pencils. He knew she wanted another letter.

62

Next, he pulled out a picture of his grandmother. He noticed she was sitting with a cat and two kittens. He thought for a moment and laughed. Now his grandmother would have to find a new name for her cat—in Korea, Juno was a boy's name, not a girl's.

Then he pulled out a small toy plane.

Juno smiled. His grandmother was coming to visit.

"Maybe she'll bring her cat when she comes to visit," Juno said to Sam as he climbed into bed. "Maybe you two will be friends."

Soon Juno was fast asleep. And when he dreamed that night, he dreamed about a faraway place, a village just outside Seoul, where his grandmother, whose gray hair sat on top of her head like a powdered doughnut, was sipping her morning tea.

The cool air feels crisp against her cheek. Crisp enough to **crackle**, he dreams, like the golden leaves which cover the persimmon garden.

Getting in touch with
Soyung and Susan

Author

Soyung Pak was born in South Korea, but she does not remember very much about it. She moved to the United States when she was just two years old. Like Juno,

Soyung had a grandmother who lived in South Korea. Soyung remembers playing in her American backyard. It was a lot like Juno's yard, with a nice, big tree.

Other books by Soyung Pak: *A Place to Grow* and *Sumi's First Day of School Ever*

Illustrator

Susan Kathleen Hartung says she's been drawing ever since she could hold a crayon. Unlike Juno, who used paper, Susan would draw on any surface she could find. Susan's parents were not too happy about that. But when they saw how much she loved to draw, they encouraged her to study art.

LOG ON Find out more about Soyung Pak and Susan Kathleen Hartung at **www.macmillanmh.com**

Write About It

Juno and his grandmother enjoyed getting letters. If you could get a letter from anyone in the world, from whom would it be? Why would you enjoy that?

Comprehension Check

Retell the Story

Use your Character Web to help you retell the story of *Dear Juno*. Describe the characters of Juno and his grandmother based on things they did in the story.

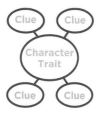

Think and Compare

1. Use your Character Web to tell about Juno and his grandmother. How do Juno and his grandmother feel about each other? How can you tell? **Analyze Story Structure: Plot, Character, Setting**

2. Why couldn't Juno read the letter his grandmother wrote? How was he able to understand her message anyway? Use story details in your answer. **Evaluate**

3. What items would you put in an **envelope** to send to a faraway relative in order to tell about your life? Explain your choices. **Apply**

4. What are some problems that can happen when relatives live far from each other? Explain your answer. **Analyze**

5. Read "Mail for Matty" on pages 40–41. How are Matty and Juno alike? How are they both surprised at the end of each story? Use details from both selections in your answer. **Reading/Writing Across Texts**

How We Keep in Touch

by Eric Michaels

When your great-grandparents were young, the world was very different. People did not have the kind of **technology** that we have today to **communicate** with each other. Things such as cell phones and computers were not yet invented. It took longer for people to get news about each other.

Today's technology makes it easier and faster to stay close to people.

How Communicating Has Changed

Reading a Time Line

Read the time line from left to right. Use the dates to find out when events took place.

1800

1850

1843–1844

First telegraph line built

1843

First fax machine

1860–1861

Mail delivered by Pony Express

Back Then

Long ago, people wrote letters to stay in touch. From 1860–1861, some letters were carried by the Pony Express. Only the fastest horseback riders were hired to carry letters and packages across the country. Then trains began to carry the mail from city to city. By the early 1900s, airplanes were a faster way to carry mail across the country and around the world.

Sometimes a message had to reach someone almost immediately. Telegraphs were machines that could send signals in a special code over an electric line.

1876
First long distance phone calls

1900

1911
First airmail flight in the U.S.

1950

1973
First cell phone call

1975–1977
First personal computers

2000

1990s
First personal computers link to the Internet

Here and Now

As times changed, the tools we use to communicate have **improved**. New inventions have made it easy to contact friends and family within seconds!

Telephones came into use in the late 1800s. They were very different than the phones you use now. Early phones did not have dials. Many people shared phone lines with others. The shared lines were called party lines.

Modern phones can do so many things. Wireless phones can be carried with us wherever we travel. Some phones let you play games, get text messages, and even take pictures! These **images** can be sent to other wireless phones.

The fax machine was patented in 1843, but it came into regular use in the 1930s. A fax machine sends images on paper as electric signals. Then, another machine receives the signals and prints them. Many offices and homes have fax machines.

Computers have made some of the biggest changes in communication. The Internet sends e-mail messages around the world in seconds! Some families have their own Web sites. They can post pictures and family news so everyone can be kept up-to-date.

Although new technology helps us stay in touch with each other, many people still enjoy sending and getting letters. With so many ways to communicate, it's easy to find your favorite way to keep in touch.

Connect and Compare

1. Look at the time line on pages 68–69. What two inventions became popular between the years 1950 and 2000? **Reading a Time Line**

2. Why do you think so many people now use computers to stay in touch with each other? **Analyze**

3. Think about this article and *Dear Juno*. In what other ways could Juno and his grandmother have communicated with each other? **Reading/Writing Across Texts**

Social Studies Activity

Do research and make a time line with important dates to show how the telephone has changed from the 1800s to the present day.

LOG ON Find out more about communication at **www.macmillanmh.com**

Write a Friendly Letter

Writing

Sentence Fluency

A sentence is a group of words that tells a complete idea. Be sure to write in complete sentences.

My name is Keri. Here is a letter I wrote to my friend Chris. I wrote about something that happened to me.

I used complete sentences.

71 Clarkson Street

Detroit, MI 56789

July 10, 20--

Dear Chris,

My mom took me to a professional soccer game on Sunday. It was so much fun! We ate hot dogs and popcorn. Our team made lots of goals. They won the game by a score of 5 to 2. The best thing happened after the game! I met my favorite player.

Will you come with us next time?

Your friend,

Keri

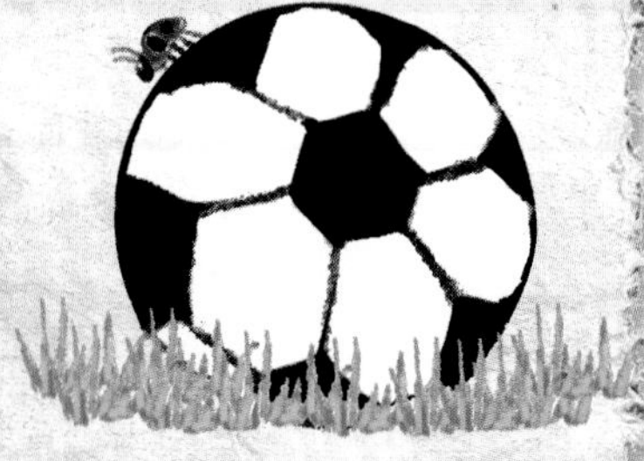

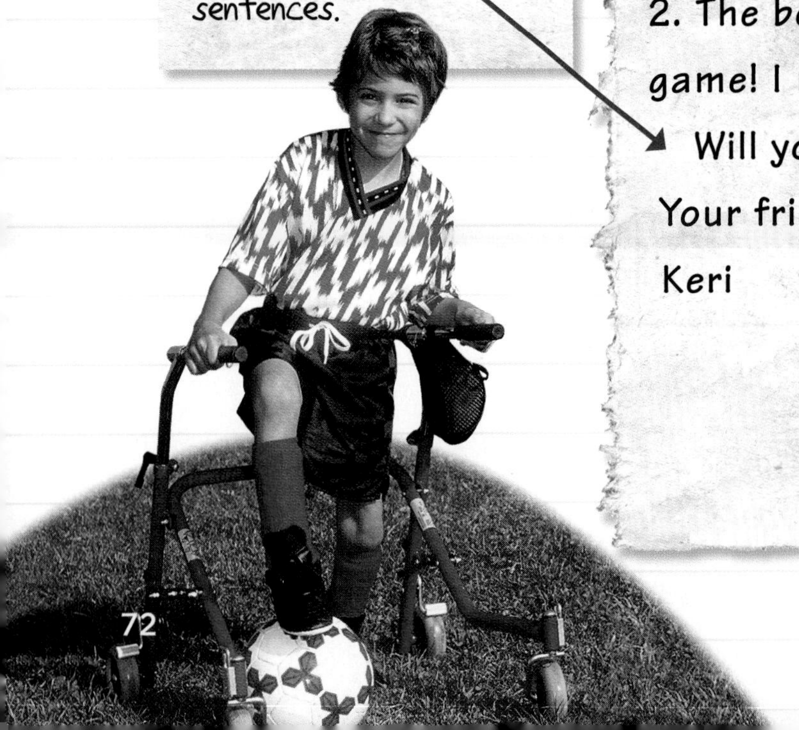

Your Turn

Write a friendly letter to a family member or a friend. Describe a recent experience you have had. It may be about something that happened at school or at home. It may be about something you did with your friends. Be sure that every sentence expresses a complete thought. Use the Writer's Checklist to check your writing.

Writer's Checklist

✓ **Ideas and Content:** Is my message clear?

✓ **Organization:** Did I include a greeting, closing, and signature in my letter?

✓ **Voice:** Is the tone of my writing friendly?

✓ **Word Choice:** Did I choose words that fit?

☐ **Sentence Fluency:** Did I write complete sentences and avoid sentence fragments?

✓ **Conventions:** Did I use commas after the greeting and closing of my letter? Did I use periods after statements and exclamation points after exclamations?

Talk About It

What makes a group of people a community?

LOG ON Find out more about communities at www.macmillanmh.com

Building Communities

Jacob Lawrence's painting of schoolgirls

Home Sweet Harlem

During the 1920s, Harlem became a famous center for African Americans. Thousands of African Americans moved from the South to this New York City **neighborhood**. Many artists, performers, and writers called Harlem their home.

In 1924, 7-year-old Jacob Lawrence moved to Harlem with his mother. When he moved there, he began to dream. That's when he decided to learn how to paint. African Americans weren't allowed to attend special art schools then. Lawrence had to be **content** to learn art at a class after school. After years of studying art in Harlem, Lawrence became a famous artist.

Many other famous artists, entertainers, musicians, and poets lived in Harlem, too. For the first time in U.S. history, the world of black artists was recognized. The people of Harlem worked together to make their dreams come true.

Jacob Lawrence in his studio

LOG ON Find out more about Jacob Lawrence at www.macmillanmh.com

Saving a Language

By teaching kids the Cherokee language, Lost City Elementary School in Oklahoma is **addressing** a problem. Not many people speak Cherokee anymore, so the school wants to save the language.

"If we don't learn Cherokee, our grandsons won't know it," says Crystal Braden, a 13-year-old student. At Lost City School, everyone works together to keep their language alive.

Students study Cherokee at Lost City School.

Girls at School

These Iraqi girls are now able to go to school. A few years ago that was impossible.

Did you know that 121 million children around the world do not go to school? About 54 percent, or more than half of those kids, are girls.

When schooling is not free, poor families can often afford to send only one child to school. They often **resort** to sending a boy.

UNICEF is the United Nations Children's Fund. It works to protect children's rights in communities all over the world. UNICEF is working on behalf of free education in 25 countries. That way, every girl and boy will be able to make the grade.

Whose Habitat Is It?

What happens when human communities expand into wildlife habitats?

A black bear visits someone's backyard.

They come out of the woods when darkness falls. They are hungry, and they are not picky eaters. Black bears are **content** munching on birdseed, chicken bones, or other food scraps.

"It's been going on for about three years," says Gregg Baker, 49. He lives in Margaretville, New York, at the edge of a forest. One night he woke to the sound of banging. "I went running downstairs," says Baker. "There was a bear on the picnic table attempting to get in the kitchen window."

78

Animals are making themselves at home in human neighborhoods. In Georgia, alligators have made a splash in **neighborhood** pools. One even strolled down a sidewalk in Savannah! In Big Pine Key, a Florida island, deer eat flowerbeds. In parts of New Jersey, black bears are getting too close for comfort. According to one resident, "Bears don't belong here. People do."

Road to Wildlife

Why is life in some U.S. neighborhoods getting wilder? New homes are popping up in places where wildlife lives. Each year, about two million acres of open space are turned into housing, roads, and buildings. This is called urban sprawl.

Elk graze peacefully outside a house near Yellowstone National Park.

79

In Florida, problem alligators are trapped and removed.

A snowman's carrot nose attracts a white-tailed deer.

A bear cub dashes across the street in downtown Durango, Colorado.

Urban sprawl upsets the plants and animals that live in an area. When humans move into a habitat, animals and plants lose some of the land and water they need to survive. This can cause animals and plants to become endangered, or even extinct.

A Shrinking World

When big highways or other structures are built on their land, animals may run out of food to eat. Some species must look for food to survive. Many animals, like the bears in New Jersey, **resort** to roaming through neighborhoods for tasty treats.

Scientists say we can protect animals by changing the way we build new communities. For example, in the Florida Everglades, builders are **addressing** the problem by making special bridges and tunnels so that alligators, panthers, and bobcats can cross roads safely. Deer and other animals have also been protected by nature-friendly building projects.

Michael Klemens works for the Wildlife Conservation Society. He helps city planners build a better future. "We know more than we did 20 years ago," he says. "We can take that knowledge and make better decisions."

Critters in Trouble

In nearly every state, animals are threatened by development. This map shows states in which animals are threatened by urban sprawl.

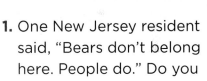

MAP KEY
- Alligator
- White-tailed deer
- Key deer
- Black bear

Alaska

Hawaii

WA, MT, ND, MN, OR, ID, WY, SD, IA, WI, MI, NH, VT, ME, NY, MA, RI, CT, NJ, DE, MD, D.C., PA, OH, WV, VA, IN, IL, KY, NC, NV, UT, CO, NE, MO, KS, TN, SC, CA, AZ, NM, OK, AK, MS, AL, GA, TX, LA, FL

Key deer

Alligator

White-tailed deer

Black bear

Think and Compare

STRATEGY SKILL

1. One New Jersey resident said, "Bears don't belong here. People do." Do you agree or disagree with that statement? Explain your reasons.

2. What animals are mentioned in this article?

3. What is urban sprawl?

4. How are the people at Lost City School and wildlife experts around the country addressing their problems?

All Are Equal: It's the Law!

Linda Brown in 1951

In the early 1950s, black students and white students went to separate schools in many states. That unfair practice changed in 1954. The parents of Linda Brown, 7, wanted to send their daughter to an all-white school in Topeka, Kansas. The school was just a few blocks from where the Browns lived. Instead, Linda had to travel two miles to a school for African Americans only.

In 1951, Linda's father went to court to tell Linda's story. On May 17, 1954, the Supreme Court ruled that segregation—separating people because of their color—in public schools was against the law. Schools across the country had to integrate—allow black and white students to go to school together.

Many years later, Linda Brown talked about that famous day. "I remember seeing tears of joy in the eyes of my father as he hugged us," she said. That victory made it possible for all kids, no matter what their skin color is, to have an excellent education.

Linda Brown's Triumph

1944: Linda is born on May 14.

1948: The Brown family moves to Topeka, Kansas.

1951: Linda Brown cannot go to an all-white school.

1954: The Supreme Court listens to Linda's father and rules that all schools must be integrated.

1956: Linda Brown enters an integrated junior high school.

Go On ▶

Directions: Answer the questions.

1. **What did Linda Brown's parents want?**

   A They wanted to send their daughter to an all-white school.

   B They wanted a new school to be built in their neighborhood.

   C They wanted the school district to buy more buses.

   D They wanted to leave Topeka, Kansas.

2. **Which word means "separating people because of the color of their skin"?**

   A integration

   B division

   C segregation

   D separation

Tip
Look for key words.

3. **Look at the time line. What year did the Brown family move to Kansas?**

   A 1944

   B 1948

   C 1954

   D 1956

4. **Why do you think it took three years to change the law? Use details from the article in your answer.**

5. **Summarize the main idea of the article. Use the time line and details from the article to help you.**

Write to a Prompt

In the selection "Whose Habitat Is It?" you read about what happens to wildlife when new highways are built. Suppose a highway were being built in your community. What might happen? What could you do to help? Use details from the article to support your answer.

I used details to support my main idea.

A Better Highway

A new highway is something people usually like. Highways help people travel from place to place more quickly. Sometimes highways hurt animals that live in neighborhoods where highways are built. If the new highway is built, many animals will lose their homes. Another problem is that animals could try to cross the highway. That is dangerous for the animals and for people in cars. I have an idea for solving this problem. The highway should have fences to keep animals off. It should also have bridges or tunnels so animals can go from one side to the other. That way, the highway would be good for people, and it would not be so bad for animals.

Writing Prompt

How would you feel if new construction were taking place in your community? Would you agree with the builders or try to save the animals? Use information from "Whose Habitat Is It?" to support your answer.

Writer's Checklist

- ☑ Ask yourself, who is my audience?
- ☑ Think about your purpose for writing.
- ☑ Plan your writing before beginning.
- ☑ Use details to support your main idea.
- ☑ Be sure your ideas are clear and organized.
- ☑ Use your best spelling, grammar, and punctuation.

Antarctic Life

Talk About It

Antarctica is a cold, icy place. What kinds of things do you think can live there?

LOG ON Find out more about Antarctic life at **www.macmillanmh.com**

Life in Antarctica

by Kenji Foster

The coldest and iciest place on Earth is Antarctica. There, the temperature hardly ever gets above freezing, even in the summer. Believe it or not, some things can live in such a frozen land.

Plants

In the coldest months, a **fierce** wind **whips** the air across Antarctica. Those strong, blowing winds make the air so chilly that there is little rain. Simple plants without leaves, such as mosses and lichens [LY-kihnz], are the only kinds that can live in Antarctica. These plants grow on rocks near the coast where it is a little warmer.

Seabirds

Penguins, Antarctic terns, and brown skuas are three kinds of birds that live in Antarctica. If you listen closely, you may hear a penguin's bark as it **echoes**– bouncing off the icy land and softly repeating. Each penguin **shuffles** along the ice. Then they get together in a **huddle**, or tight group, to keep warm. New chicks have a layer of soft, fluffy feathers called **down**. As they grow into **junior** penguins, they begin to develop stiff, waterproof feathers. Now they can swim in cold water. While penguins live in Antarctica all year, the terns and the brown skuas only visit in the summer.

Seals and Whales

Blue whales, humpback whales, and southern right whales spend their summers in Antarctica as well. They have plenty of fat to keep them warm. Leopard seals, as well as Ross, Weddell, and crabeater seals, rely on thick fur for warmth. Crabeater seals travel well on land, but leopard, Ross, and Weddell seals move fastest when they stay **down** below the surface of the icy water.

Reread for **Comprehension**

STRATEGY SKILL

Summarize

Main Idea and Details

The main idea of an article or paragraph explains what the article or paragraph is about. The details tell about the main idea.

A Main Idea Chart can help you summarize an article or paragraph. Reread the selection to find the main idea and the details that tell about it.

Main Idea	Details

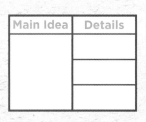

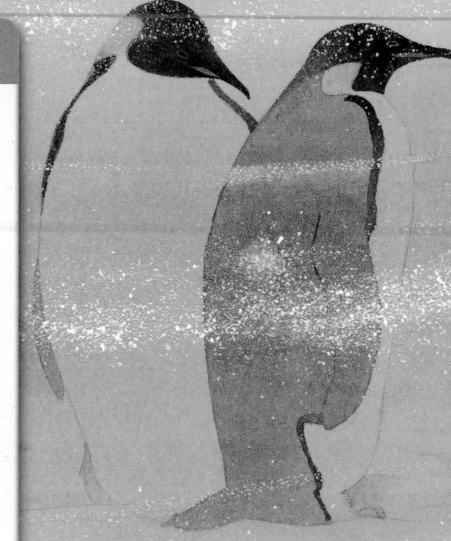

Comprehension

Genre

Narrative Nonfiction is a story or account about actual living things.

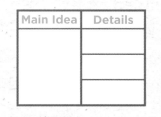

Summarize

Main Idea and Details

As you read, use your Main Idea Chart.

Main Idea	Details

Read to Find Out

How does the father penguin take care of the penguin chick?

Penguin Chick

By Betty Tatham
Illustrated by Helen K. Davie

Award Winning Selection

A **fierce** wind howls. It **whips** snow across the ice. Here, a female emperor penguin has just laid an egg. It is the only egg she will lay this year.

Most birds build nests for their eggs. But on the ice in Antarctica, there are no twigs or leaves. There is no grass or mud. Nothing to build a nest with. Nothing but snow and ice.

The new penguin father uses his beak to scoop the egg onto his webbed feet.

He tucks it under his feather-covered skin, into a special place called a brood patch. The egg will be as snug and warm there as if it were in a sleeping bag.

One of the penguin parents must stay with the egg to keep it warm. But where penguins lay their eggs, there is no food for them to eat.

The penguin father is bigger and fatter than the mother. He can live longer without food. So the father penguin stays with the egg while the mother travels to the sea to find food.

The two parents sing together before the mother penguin leaves.

Along with many other penguins, the mother penguin leaves the rookery, where she laid her egg.

The mother walks or slides on her belly. This is called tobogganing. She uses her flippers and webbed feet to push herself forward over ice and snow.

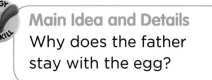

Main Idea and Details
Why does the father stay with the egg?

Because it's winter in Antarctica, water near the shore is frozen for many miles. After three days the mother penguin comes to the end of the ice.

FISH

SQUID

KRILL

She dives into the water to hunt for fish, squid,
and tiny shrimplike creatures called krill.

Back at the rookery, the penguin fathers form a group called a **huddle**. They stand close together for warmth. Each one keeps his own egg warm.

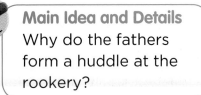

Main Idea and Details
Why do the fathers form a huddle at the rookery?

For two months the penguin father always keeps his egg on his feet. When he walks, he **shuffles** his feet so the egg doesn't roll away. He sleeps standing up. He has no food to eat, but the fat on his body keeps him alive.

Finally he feels the chick move inside the egg. The chick pecks and pecks and pecks. In about three days the egg cracks open.

The chick is wet. But soon his soft feathers, called **down**, dry and become fluffy and gray. The father still keeps the chick warm in the brood patch. Sometimes the chick pokes his head out. But while he's so little, he must stay covered. And he must stay on his father's feet. Otherwise the cold would kill him.

The father talks to the chick in his trumpet voice. The chick answers with a whistle.

The father's trumpet call **echoes** across the ice. The penguin mother is on her way back to the rookery, but she can't hear him. She's still too far away. If the mother doesn't come back soon with food, the chick will die.

Two days pass before the mother can hear the father penguin's call.

At last the mother arrives at the rookery. She cuddles close to her chick and trumpets to him. He whistles back. With her beak she brushes his soft gray down.

The mother swallowed many fish before she left the ocean. She brings some of this food back up from her stomach and feeds her chick. She has enough food to keep him fed for weeks. He stays on her feet and snuggles into her brood patch.

The father is very hungry, so he travels to open water. There he dives to hunt for food. Weeks later the father returns with more food for the chick.

Each day the parents preen, or brush, the chick's downy coat with their beaks. This keeps the down fluffy and keeps the chick warm.

As the chick gets bigger, he and the other chicks no longer need to stay on their parents' feet. Instead they stay together to keep warm.

This group of chicks is called a crèche, or a nursery. The chick now spends most of his time here. But he still rushes to his mother or father to be fed when either one comes back from the ocean.

Sometimes the chick and the other young penguins dig their beaks into the ice to help them walk up a slippery hill. They toboggan **down** fast on their fluffy bellies.

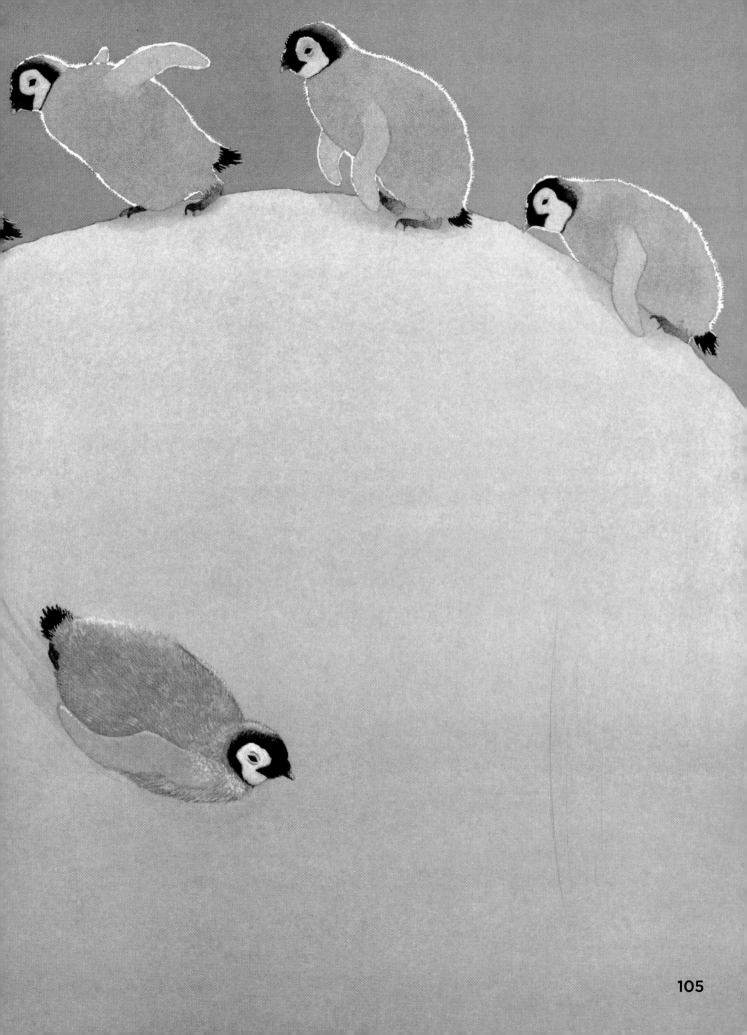

The chick grows and grows. After five months, he has grown into a **junior** penguin. He is old enough to travel to the ocean.

WINTER		SPRING	
August	September	October	

Now he has a waterproof coat of feathers, instead of fluffy down. He can swim in the icy cold ocean because his feathers keep him dry and warm.

November	December	SUMMER January

The young penguin spends most of his time in the water. He swims, flapping his flippers as if he were flying underwater. He uses his webbed feet to steer wherever he wants to go.

He catches a fish with his beak and swallows it headfirst.

Now the young penguin can catch his own food and take care of himself. In about five years he'll find a mate. Then he'll take care of his own egg until the chick can hatch.

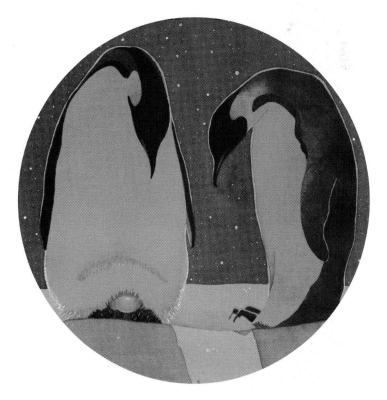

Chill Out with Betty and Helen!

Author

Betty Tatham likes writing nonfiction books about animals for children. She became interested in writing after years of teaching children to enjoy nature and write their own stories. Betty works hard at being an author. She has taken writing classes and attended special conferences for writers.

Other books by Betty Tatham: *How Animals Communicate* and *How Animals Play*

© Alex Lowy.

Illustrator

Helen K. Davie has chilly memories of her work on this story. She went to Sea World in San Diego and spent time in the emperor penguins' frozen habitat. Helen got an up-close look at the birds so she could draw them better.

Write About It

These penguins live in Antarctica, but they have some things in common with us. How are people and penguins alike?

LOG ON Find out more about Betty Tatham and Helen K. Davie at **www.macmillanmh.com**

Comprehension Check

Retell the Story

STRATEGY SKILL

Use your Main Idea Chart to help you retell *Penguin Chick*. Include the most important ideas and supporting details about the life of an emperor penguin chick.

Main Idea	Details

Think and Compare

STRATEGY SKILL

1. Describe Antarctica, the home of emperor penguins. What makes it hard for penguin chicks to survive in this **fierce**, cold place? **Summarize: Main Idea and Details**

2. What would happen if the mother and father penguins left the chick at the same time to get food? **Synthesize**

3. Emperor penguins work as a team. Discuss the ways you work as a member of a team. **Apply**

4. In what ways are emperor penguins like other animals and their young? **Evaluate**

5. What is the common main idea in "Life in Antarctica" and *Penguin Chick*? Use details from both selections to support your answer. **Reading/Writing Across Texts**

Antarctic Anthem

Poetry

Poetry uses elements such as rhyme, rhythm, and repetition to express feelings and ideas.

Literary Elements

Rhythmic Patterns are series of stressed and unstressed syllables.

Imagery is the use of words to create a picture in the reader's mind.

Breaking "Antarctica" into syllables and repeating it again and again creates a rhythmic pattern in the poem.

At the bottom of the planet
Lies a land of ice and granite:
Ant · arc · ti · ca! Ant · arc · ti · ca!
Where winter days are dark-tica.
It's the continent of our birth;
It's the coldest place on earth:
Ant · arc · ti · ca! Ant · arc · ti · ca!
You'd better wear your park-tica,
Or the brutal, blasting blizzards
Will freeze your beaks and gizzards.
Ant · arc · ti · ca! Ant · arc · ti · ca!

Come visit on a lark-tica!
We'll snuggle in the snow
When it's thirty-five below.
Ant · arc · ti · ca! Ant · arc · ti · ca!
It's grander than New York-tica.
Skyscraping icebergs roam
All across the frosty foam
In our sweet Antarctic home.

— *Judy Sierra*

This line uses imagery to paint a picture of icebergs being as big as skyscrapers.

Connect and Compare

1. Which words in this poem help form an image of Antarctica? **Imagery**

2. An anthem is the official song of a country or place. How are the words of "Antarctic Anthem" like a song? **Evaluate**

3. Compare "Antarctic Anthem" to *Penguin Chick.* Which selection gives you more information about life in Antarctica? Explain. **Reading/Writing Across Texts**

LOG ON Find out more about lyric poems at **www.macmillanmh.com**

Write an
Acrostic Poem

Writing

Word Choice

A writer chooses words to create a clear and accurate picture for readers. Choose just the right words to describe how something looks, acts, sounds, feels, or smells.

I wrote an acrostic poem. When you put the first letter of each line together, it spells penguins.

I used words that create a picture.

All About Emperor Penguins

by Keisha J.

Peck to get out of eggs
Eggs balance on father's feet
No nest
Glide on bellies over snow
Unique
Ice walkers
Need waterproof feathers
Sleep standing up

Your Turn

Write an acrostic poem about an animal. It may be an animal you have seen in a zoo. It may be an animal you have learned about in books or on television. Be sure to use words that create a "picture" of the animal. Use the Writer's Checklist to check your writing.

Writer's Checklist

☑ **Ideas and Content:** Did I include details that are interesting?

☑ **Organization:** Do the first words in each line begin with the correct letters?

☑ **Voice:** Did I use language that shows how I feel about the topic?

 ☐ **Word Choice:** Did I use precise words that describe the animal?

☑ **Sentence Fluency:** Does the poem flow well and sound good when I read it out loud?

☑ **Conventions:** Did I check my spelling?

People and Their Pets

Talk About It

Pets are fun. In what ways is owning a pet a big responsibility?

LOG ON Find out more about people and their pets at **www.macmillanmh.com**

Choosing a Pet

by Michael Teras

Luis was excited because he was going to get a pet. He thought about all of the kinds of animals he liked. But which pet would be **perfect** for him and his family? Finding the right pet would be a **challenge**, but he was ready to try.

At the Pet Store

"How about getting a dog, Mom?" Luis asked. "Look at how playful this one is. It would be a great pal!"

"It is lively and friendly," Mrs. Santiago laughed. "And look at its shiny fur! It looks very **healthy**. A dog would be fun and friendly. But could we **satisfy** a dog's needs? I work during the day and you're in school. No one would be home during the day to **manage** its care."

Problems with Pets

Mr. Stein, the store owner, tried to help. "Dogs like to spend time with their owners," said Mr. Stein. "Some dogs get upset when they're left alone."

Luis sighed. "We can't get a dog then. I guess we can **scratch** it off our list."

"How about a cat?" asked Mr. Stein.

"Ah-choo!" Mrs. Santiago sneezed. "Cats are very cute, but I have an allergy. Cats make me sneeze."

"What's left, Mom?" Luis asked.

A Good Match

"Cats and dogs are very popular pets," said Mr. Stein. "But there are other wonderful pets, such as rabbits, guinea pigs, and fish."

Luis petted a small, spotted rabbit. "Its fur is so soft. I like its wiggly, black nose!"

"Rabbits don't mind being alone. And they have a small **appetite**. Rabbits eat very little compared to big dogs," said Mr. Stein. "Plus, they don't **scratch** the furniture in order to sharpen their claws, as cats sometimes do."

"Luis," Mrs. Santiago said, "I think we found the right pet for both of us!"

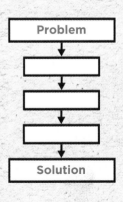

Reread for **Comprehension**

Analyze Story Structure
Problem and Solution
A story's plot begins with a character who has a problem. The problem is what the character wants to do, find out, or change. The solution is how the problem is solved.

A Problem and Solution Chart can help you understand story structure. Reread the selection to find the problem, three ways they tried to solve it, and the solution.

Problem
Solution

Comprehension

Genre

Humorous Fiction is a made-up story written to make readers laugh.

Analyze Story Structure

Problem and Solution

As you read, use your Problem and Solution Chart.

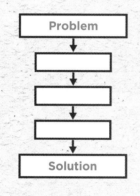

```
┌─────────────────┐
│     Problem     │
└─────────────────┘
         ↓
┌─────────────────┐
│                 │
└─────────────────┘
         ↓
┌─────────────────┐
│                 │
└─────────────────┘
         ↓
┌─────────────────┐
│                 │
└─────────────────┘
         ↓
┌─────────────────┐
│    Solution     │
└─────────────────┘
```

Read to Find Out

How does Elizabeth solve her problem?

The Perfect Pet

Award Winning Author

by

Margie Palatini

illustrated by

Bruce Whatley

Elizabeth really, really, *really* wanted a pet. Her parents really, really, *really* did not.

They gave her a plant instead.

Mind you, it was a very good-looking plant, as cactus plants go. And it had quite a prickly sense of humor.

Elizabeth named it Carolyn, which seemed to suit it just fine. It was absolutely no trouble and it was a very good listener.

Snuggling was a bit of a **challenge**. However, Elizabeth did **manage** a quick hug now and then.

Elizabeth really, really did like the plant … but, she still really, really, *really* wanted a pet.

And she had a plan.

The Element of Surprise

"So, how about a horse?"

"Huh? What? Who?" said Father.

"Who? What? Huh?" said Mother.

"I could ride it. Give it carrots. Lumps of sugar. A horse would be the **perfect** pet. Whaddya say?"

Father yawned. "A horse is too big."

Mother sighed. "Our yard is too small."

"Why, it would eat us out of house and home," said Father.

"A horse is not *quite* perfect, dear," said Mother, going back to sleep.

"Not *quite* perfect," said Father sleepily.

Scratch the horse.

Catch Them Off Guard

"What about a dog?"

"Huh? What? Who?" said Father as he stood in front of the mirror shaving.

"Who? What? Huh?" said Mother, peeking from behind the shower curtain and dripping soapy water.

"I could take it for walks. Teach it tricks. Feed it treats. Play fetch. A dog would be the perfect pet. Whaddya think?"

Father spit shaving cream. "Dogs bark. They're much too loud."

Mother grabbed a towel. "They jump all over the furniture."

"A dog is not *quite* perfect, Elizabeth," said Father as he shaved.

"Not *quite* perfect," called Mother from the shower.

Forget Fido.

The Full Stomach

Burp.

"You know what would hit the spot right about now?" asked Elizabeth. "I'm thinking … a cat."

"Huh? What? Who?" said Father.

"Who? What? Huh?" said Mother.

"A cat could lick the plates. Curl up in my lap. Drink leftover milk. And we'd always know what to do with all that extra string. A cat would be the perfect pet. So … how about it?"

Father picked up the newspaper. "Cats **scratch**."

Mother cleared the table. "Cats shed all over."

"A cat is definitely *not* the perfect pet," said Father.

"Achoo! I'm sneezing already," said Mother.

Cross off kitty.

Problem and Solution
How is Elizabeth trying to solve her problem?

Go for Broke

"How about a bird?
        Bunny?
        Turtle?
        Fish?
        Guinea pig?
        Rat?
        Any? All?
Take your pick!" said Elizabeth.

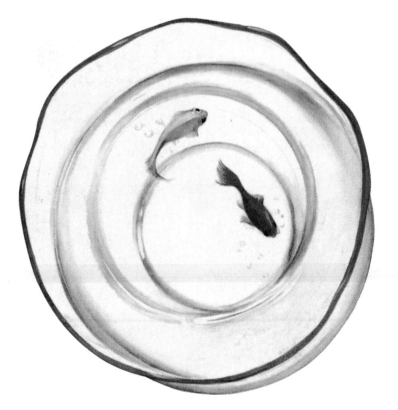

Her parents looked at each other.

"Nope."

"Afraid not."

"Not quite."

"Too fishy."

"Uh-uh."

"Don't even go there."

"What's left?"
moaned Elizabeth.

Doug

Elizabeth was thinking she would never ever find the really, really, *really* perfect pet, when … what do you know? She really, really did.

In fact, she almost stepped on it.

Right there on her rug. A bug.

Elizabeth picked him up.

She held him in her hand. Looked him in the eyes.

He wasn't too big. He most definitely was not too loud.

He couldn't jump on the furniture. Didn't scratch. Didn't shed. And how much food could he possibly eat?

He was the perfect pet.

Carolyn totally agreed.

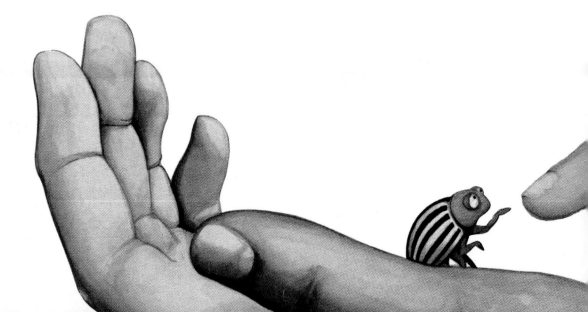

Snug

Doug moved right in to the lovely house in the corner of Elizabeth's room. It had everything a bug could possibly want and more. Including his very own cactus plant, as Carolyn was only a hop, skip, and jump away. He truly enjoyed sunning himself in her sand.

Of course, Elizabeth provided him with enough crumbs to **satisfy** any growing bug's **appetite**.

As expected, their relationship was a *tad* different than the usual.

Doug could not give Elizabeth a pony ride. She could not take him for a walk.

He could not catch a ball or fetch, no matter how many times they practiced.

And try as he might, Doug just couldn't get the hang of playing with string.

But he was very helpful with homework. (He always knew where to put a decimal or a period.)

And he loved snuggling up with Elizabeth each night for a story. What more could you ask? He was perfect.

Problem and Solution
How do you think Elizabeth's parents will feel about the pet she chose?

THERE AIN'T NO BUGS ON ME

Unsnugged

With all those crumbs and plenty of sun, Doug grew by leaps and bounds. He was one big, **healthy** bug … and then some.

The only trouble really, really, *really* came one Saturday morning, many weeks later. Elizabeth's mother came into her bedroom to get the laundry and …

"THERE'S A BUG IN THAT BED!" she screamed.

"A bug!" shouted Father, ready to swat.

"That's Doug," said Elizabeth very protectively. "He's my pet."

Her parents looked at each other. "Pet?"

"Pet," said Elizabeth. "Just like you wanted. He's not big like a horse. He isn't loud like a dog. He doesn't jump on furniture, scratch, or shed. And he hardly eats a thing."

"But, a *bug*?" asked Father.

"A *bug*?" repeated Mother.

"*Doug*," said Elizabeth. "And he's perfect."

One Big Happy Family

"Think we should have said 'yes' to the dog?" whispered Father to Mother.

Mother shrugged. "I don't know. We have more room on the couch with the bug."

Elizabeth smiled and tossed Doug a piece of popcorn.

The Perfect Pair!

Author

Margie Palatini got the idea for this story from the games she used to play when she was Elizabeth's age. Margie would pretend she was a horse, dog, or even a cat. Speaking of cats, Margie has her very own! His name is JD.

Margie Palatini

Other books by Margie Palatini: *Mary Had a Little Ham* and *Bedhead*

Bruce Whatley

Illustrator

Bruce Whatley illustrated this story, but he writes stories, too. It's hard to believe that he didn't learn to read until he was 10 years old. Reading still isn't easy, but he always tries because he really loves a good story.

LOG ON Find out more about Margie Palatini and Bruce Whatley at **www.macmillanmh.com**

 **Write About It**

Elizabeth had many ideas about what a perfect pet might be. Describe your idea of a perfect pet.

Comprehension Check

Retell the Story

Use your Problem and Solution Chart to help you retell *The Perfect Pet*. Tell about Elizabeth's problem and how she tried to solve it.

Problem
Solution

Think and Compare

1. Describe one possible problem with having a pet bug. How would Elizabeth **manage** to solve that problem? **Analyze Story Structure: Problem and Solution**

2. Why did Elizabeth make a plan? How well did it work? Use story details in your answer. **Evaluate**

3. What would happen if you brought Doug home to be your pet? Explain. **Synthesize**

4. Why do you think Elizabeth didn't tell her parents about Doug? Explain your answer. **Analyze**

5. Read "Choosing a Pet" on pages 118-119. How is Luis's experience similar to Elizabeth's? How is it different? Use details from both selections in your answer. **Reading/Writing Across Texts**

Pets
True or False?

by Gillian Reed

Most of us know the usual things about pets—that dogs can bark and that cats can scratch. But sometimes we believe things without checking information. It is important to **examine**, or look closely at, facts. This is necessary when coming to a **conclusion**, or making a decision about something. For example, have you ever seen a snake at the zoo? Did it look as if it would feel cold and slimy? This is actually false. A snake's skin is dry and scaly!

Try to figure out if the statements on the next few pages are **True or False.**

True or False?
A **goldfish** opens its mouth to drink water.

False Goldfish may look as if they're drinking water, but they actually open their mouths to take in oxygen. Like people, fish need **oxygen** to live. Oxygen is a gas that is found in air and water. Fish use gills to get oxygen from water. The water enters the fish's mouth, then moves through the gills behind the fish's head. The gills remove oxygen from the water, and the water passes out of the gills.

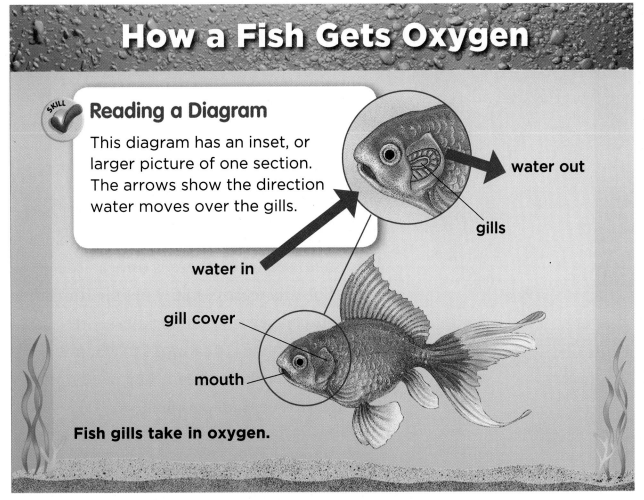

How a Fish Gets Oxygen

SKILL ✓ **Reading a Diagram**

This diagram has an inset, or larger picture of one section. The arrows show the direction water moves over the gills.

water out

gills

water in

gill cover

mouth

Fish gills take in oxygen.

True or False?
A wagging tail always means a **dog** is friendly.

False You may know that dogs wag their tails when they feel friendly. You may not know that they also wag their tails when they are excited or angry. Always be careful with dogs you don't know. Do not go near a dog unless you already have a friendly relationship with it or the owner says it is all right.

True or False?
Cats can see in total darkness.

False In the wild, cats often hunt for their food at night. They have special eyes that help them see when there is only a little light. For this reason, many people think that cats can see in total darkness. But this is not true. Cats cannot see when it is completely dark, although they need much less light to see than people need.

144

True or False?

A **guinea pig** doesn't play in the morning.

True Like many small mammals, including gerbils and hamsters, guinea pigs are **nocturnal**. That means they sleep during the day and are active at night, when they look for food. If you want to choose a guinea pig for a pet, it is better to visit a pet store in the late afternoon. That is when you can see a healthy guinea pig playing.

Connect and Compare

1. Look at the text and diagram of the fish on page 143. How does a fish get oxygen? Explain. Where are the gills found? **Reading a Diagram**

2. The next time you see a strange dog wag its tail, why should you think twice about petting it? **Analyze**

3. Think about this article and *The Perfect Pet*. What information could Elizabeth's parents have used to help convince Elizabeth that a hamster might not make a good pet? **Reading/Writing Across Texts**

Science Activity

Research an animal. Draw or trace a picture of the animal and label four parts that you learned from your research. Give your diagram a title.

LOG ON Find out more about animals at **www.macmillanmh.com**

Ideas and Content

Writers elaborate by adding important ideas and details that create a clear picture for the reader.

Write About a Pet

I wanted to tell how my cat woke me up today. Here is what I wrote.

I included fun details.

My Alarm Cat
by Harry N.

My cat Zoe is the best alarm clock in the world! This morning she woke me up again. First, she walked across my tummy. Next, she rubbed my face and started purring. Her soft whiskers tickled me. I opened my eyes, and Zoe was staring at me. I petted her for a while, and then I jumped out of bed. Waking up is a fun experience with Zoe!

Your Turn

Write a paragraph about what it may be like to take care of someone else's pet or about something that happened with your own pet. Be sure to use precise words in your paragraph. Use the Writer's Checklist to check your writing.

Writer's Checklist

☑ **Ideas and Content:** Did I add details?

☑ **Organization:** Did I use words like *first* and *next* to explain the order that things happened?

☑ **Voice:** Do the details tell how I feel? Do they make my writing more interesting?

☑ **Word Choice:** Did I choose strong, precise words to tell what happened?

☑ **Sentence Fluency:** Did I join related sentences to make compound sentences?

☑ **Conventions:** Did I use commas in compound sentences? Did I check my spelling?

Test Strategy

Think and Search
The answer is in more than one place. Keep reading to find the answer.

Evan's Welcome

by Amata Lemey

CHARACTERS:

EVAN	MR. CORTEZ	MARCO
MRS. BORDONI	RITA	TOM

Setting: An elementary school

MRS. BORDONI: Good morning! You need to go straight to your classrooms, children. (*A shy boy walks up, looking nervous.*) What is your name?

EVAN: (*Looking at the ground*) My name is Evan.

MRS. BORDONI: Welcome to Northside. I'm the principal, Mrs. Bordoni.

EVAN: (*Looks surprised*) Oh! Good morning.

MRS. BORDONI: I know you are new to our school, but you will like it here. I will take you to your classroom.

EVAN: I didn't want to move … and leave my friends.

Go On ▶

MRS. BORDONI: You will have friends here. You'll see.
(They are passed by three people dressed as a doll, a cat, and a sailor.)

MRS. BORDONI: Here's your room, 106.

MR. CORTEZ: Welcome to our class! I'm Mr. Cortez.

EVAN: *(The class looks at him. He speaks softly.)* Hello.

MR. CORTEZ: We are talking about a story we just read. Who can tell Evan what it was about?

RITA: This family moves to a new state. Their story is both funny and sad.

EVAN: *(Cheering up)* Did they like the new place?

MARCO: Not at first. But they made lots of new friends.

MR. CORTEZ: What happened to make them change their minds?

TOM: The girl from next door said she needed help. When they got to her house, a sign said, "Welcome."

MARCO: It was a surprise party for them. The whole family was laughing.

MR. CORTEZ: The neighbors made the family feel welcome.

MRS. BORDONI: *(Stands in doorway)* Evan, it's time for lunch. *(They enter lunchroom. A sign says, "Welcome Evan.")* It is hard to change schools and leave old friends. Now, we are your friends.

EVAN: *(Smiles)* I can't believe you did this for me.

(The doll, cat, and sailor carry a cake that says, "Welcome, Evan.")

EVAN: Why are the kids dressed in costumes?

MR. CORTEZ: They are characters in the class play. I believe they still need another cat.

EVAN: Could I be the cat?

MRS. BORDONI: That's exactly what we were hoping. That way you'll fit right in!

EVAN: That's great. *(He laughs.)* My biggest fear was that I wouldn't fit in. Thanks!

MRS. BORDONI: You're welcome. Now, let's eat that cake!

Go On ▶

Directions: Answer the questions.

1. **How does the information in parentheses help the plot of the play?**

   A   It tells what action should be taking place.
   B   It explains the author's point of view.
   C   It describes what the actors are wearing.
   D   It explains what the play is about.

2. **How would you describe the way Evan feels?**

   A   He is afraid because he can't find the new school.
   B   He is happy because he can wear a costume to class.
   C   He is nervous because it is his first day in a new school.
   D   He is angry because the others will not talk to him.

3. **The story tells you about Evan's welcome. What does *welcome* mean here?**

   A   a grade at school
   B   a friendly greeting and a reply to "thank you"
   C   a fancy costume and sets for a play
   D   the name of the cat

4. **Why did the class want Evan to be part of the play?**

5. **What is Evan's problem? Use details from the play to describe his problem and how it is solved.**

Writing Prompt
Write a letter to a friend telling about a problem you once faced. Explain what you did to solve your problem. Be sure to write your ideas in complete sentences.

Putting on a Performance

Talk About It

Being in a show can be exciting. Describe a favorite show you have seen. What made it special?

LOG ON Find out more about performances at **www.macmillanmh.com**

Vocabulary

decorated **gnaws**
symbol **securing**
darkened **weakest**

Antonyms

Antonyms are words that have opposite meanings. The antonym of *big* is *small*. Use a thesaurus to find an antonym for *weakest*.

The Wind and the Sun

an Aesop's Fable

retold by Jon Lory

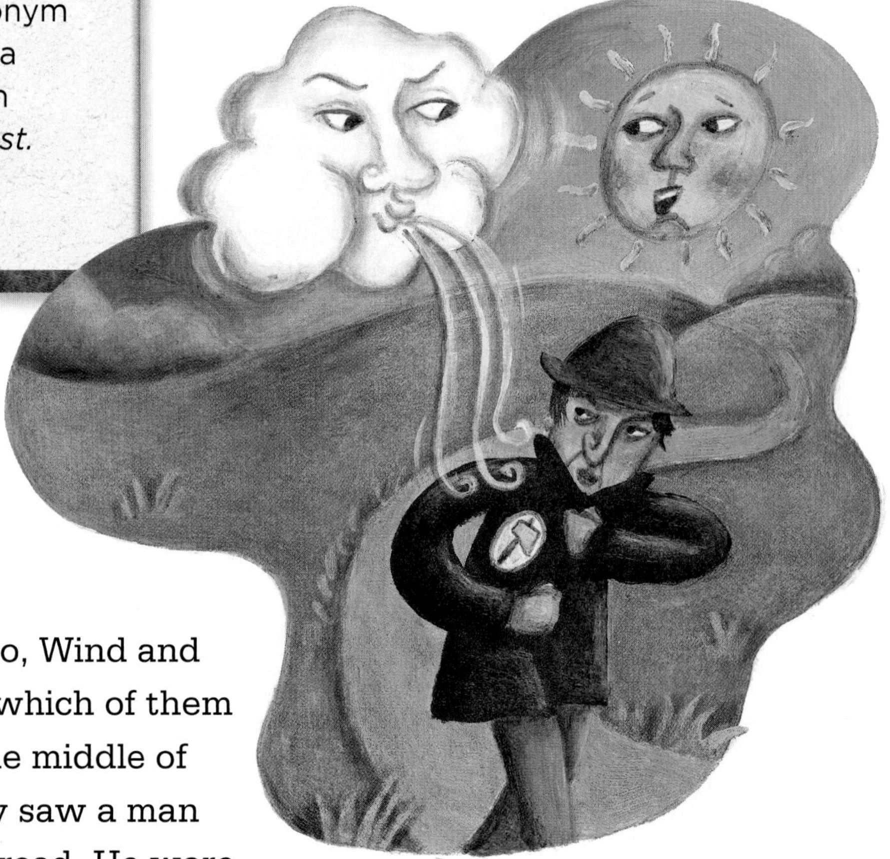

NARRATOR: Long ago, Wind and Sun argued about which of them was stronger. In the middle of the argument, they saw a man walking down the road. He wore a coat that was **decorated** with a picture of a gold axe on the front. The axe was the **symbol** of his trade. He was a woodcutter.

SUN: Let's try to get that coat off the woodcutter. Whoever can do that is stronger. You go first.

NARRATOR: Wind went first. Sun hid behind a cloud to watch from the **darkened** sky.

WIND: I will blow on the woodcutter as hard as I can. I know I can blow off that coat!

NARRATOR: So Wind blew on the woodcutter as hard as he could.

WIND: Whoooosh ... whoooosh-whoooosh ... WHOOOOOSH!

WOODCUTTER: Oh! How the cold wind **gnaws** at my bones. It is good that I have this warm coat to wrap around me.

NARRATOR: The woodcutter walked on, **securing** his coat even tighter around him. Wind gave up in despair.

WIND: That must have been the **weakest** wind I have ever made! It could not blow the coat off the woodcutter.

NARRATOR: It was now Sun's turn to try.

SUN: I will shine my rays on the woodcutter as hard as I can. I know that I will be able to remove that coat!

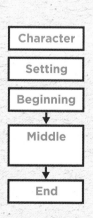

NARRATOR: So Sun shined on the woodcutter as hard as he could.

WOODCUTTER: Oh! How hot the sun shines. It is far too warm for this coat! It is good that I can take it off.

NARRATOR: So the woodcutter took off his coat, which proved that Sun was indeed stronger than Wind.

Reread for **Comprehension**

Generate Questions
Summarize
Generating, or asking, questions as you read can help you understand and summarize a story. Ask yourself what happens at the beginning, middle, and end. Your summary should tell the most important parts of a story in just a few words.

Reread "The Wind and The Sun." Use the Story Map to help you answer questions about what happens at the beginning, middle, and end of the story.

| Character |
| Setting |
| Beginning |
| ↓ |
| Middle |
| ↓ |
| End |

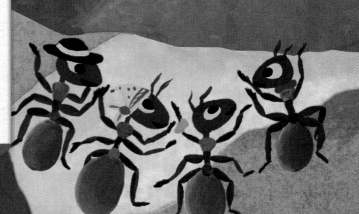

Comprehension

Genre

A **Play** is a story that is intended to be performed on a stage.

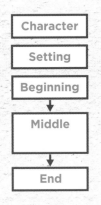

Generate Questions

Summarize

As you read, use your Story Map.

```
┌──────────────┐
│  Character   │
├──────────────┤
│   Setting    │
├──────────────┤
│  Beginning   │
└──────┬───────┘
       ↓
┌──────────────┐
│    Middle    │
│              │
└──────┬───────┘
       ↓
┌──────────────┐
│     End      │
└──────────────┘
```

Read to Find Out

How does Little Red Ant find out who is the strongest one?

THE STRONGEST ONE

A Zuni Play

By Joseph Bruchac

Illustrated by Lucia Angela Perez

Award Winning Author

THE ZUNIS are one of the people of the Southwest who dwell in pueblos, compact villages made up of multistoried buildings of adobe brick and beams. The Zunis' pueblo, which is also called Zuni, is located in present-day New Mexico. The Zunis and the other pueblo people developed means of growing their crops in the dry lands of the Southwest and are regarded as very sophisticated farmers.

The Zuni people are famous for their ceremonies, which are designed to give thanks and support to all living things, from the largest to the smallest. The Zunis are also very well-known as artists for their beautiful jewelry made of silver and turquoise.

CHARACTERS

NARRATOR

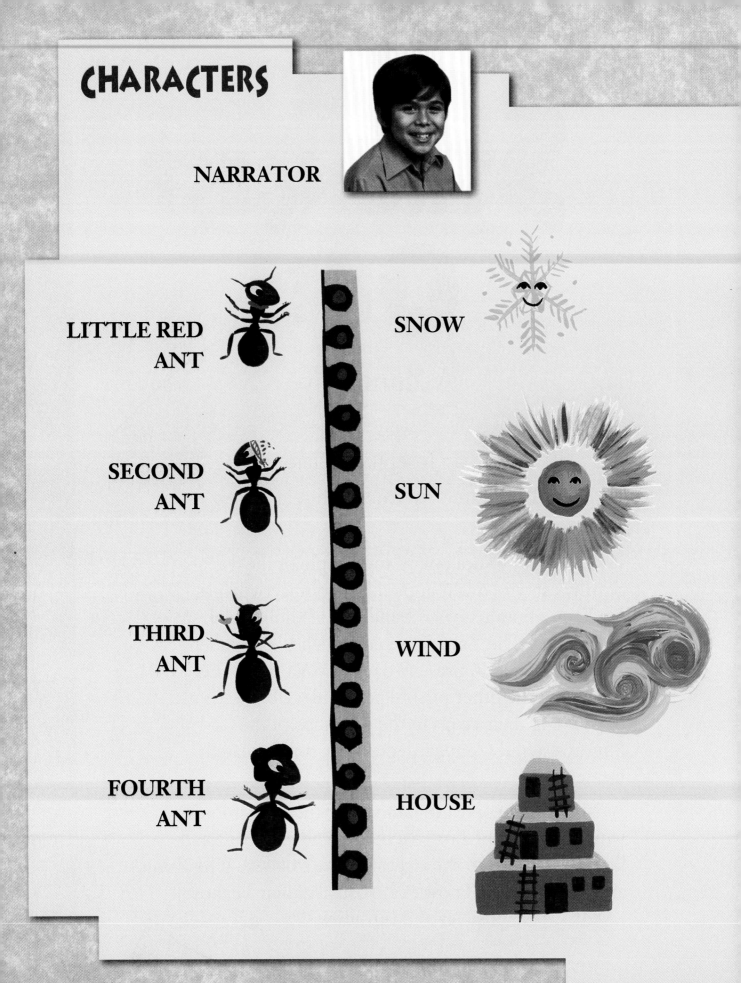

LITTLE RED
ANT

SECOND
ANT

THIRD
ANT

FOURTH
ANT

SNOW

SUN

WIND

HOUSE

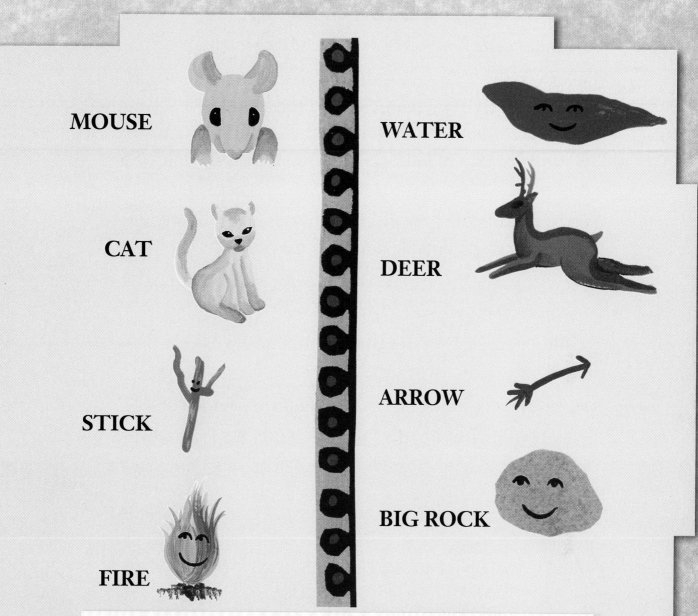

MOUSE

CAT

STICK

FIRE

WATER

DEER

ARROW

BIG ROCK

COSTUMES

NARRATOR wears long head scarf tied at the side.

THE ANTS wear feelers suggested by **securing** red pipe cleaners around a headband.

SNOW, SUN, WIND, STICK, FIRE, WATER, BIG ROCK all wear t-shirts **decorated** with their **symbol**.

HOUSE carries a large paper cutout depicting an adobe.

MOUSE, CAT, DEER can be suggested with felt tails, and felt ears secured to a headband.

ARROW carries a large cardboard arrow.

SCENE 1: INSIDE THE ANTS' HOLE

*On a **darkened** stage, the ants crouch together.*

NARRATOR: Little Red Ant lived in a hole under the Big Rock with all of its relatives. It often wondered about the world outside: Who in the world was the strongest one of all? One day in late spring Little Red Ant decided to find out.

LITTLE RED ANT: I am going to find out who is strongest. I am going to go outside and walk around.

SECOND ANT: Be careful! We ants are very small. Something might step on you.

THIRD ANT: Yes, we are the smallest and **weakest** ones of all.

FOURTH ANT: Be careful, it is dangerous out there!

LITTLE RED ANT: I will be careful. I will find out who is strongest. Maybe the strongest one can teach us how to be stronger.

Summarize
What does Little Red Ant want to find out?

Scene II: the Mesa

Ant walks back and forth onstage.

NARRATOR: So Little Red Ant went outside and began to walk around. But as Little Red Ant walked, the snow began to fall.

Snow walks onstage.

LITTLE RED ANT: Ah, my feet are cold. This snow makes everything freeze. Snow must be the strongest. I will ask. Snow, are you the strongest of all?

SNOW: No, I am not the strongest.

LITTLE RED ANT: Who is stronger than you?

SNOW: Sun is stronger. When Sun shines on me, I melt away. Here it comes!

As Sun walks onstage, Snow hurries offstage.

LITTLE RED ANT: Ah, Sun must be the strongest. I will ask. Sun, are you the strongest of all?

SUN: No, I am not the strongest.

LITTLE RED ANT: Who is stronger than you?

SUN: Wind is stronger. Wind blows the clouds across the sky and covers my face. Here it comes!

As Wind comes onstage, Sun hurries offstage with face covered in hands.

LITTLE RED ANT: Wind must be the strongest. I will ask. Wind, are you the strongest of all?

WIND: No, I am not the strongest.

LITTLE RED ANT: Who is stronger than you?

WIND: House is stronger. When I come to House, I cannot move it. I must go elsewhere. Here it comes!

As House walks onstage, Wind hurries offstage.

LITTLE RED ANT: House must be the strongest. I will ask. House, are you the strongest of all?

HOUSE: No, I am not the strongest.

LITTLE RED ANT: Who is stronger than you?

HOUSE: Mouse is stronger. Mouse comes and **gnaws** holes in me. Here it comes!

As Mouse walks onstage, House hurries offstage.

LITTLE RED ANT: Mouse must be the strongest. I will ask. Mouse, are you the strongest of all?

MOUSE: No, I am not the strongest.

LITTLE RED ANT: Who is stronger than you?

MOUSE: Cat is stronger. Cat chases me, and if Cat catches me, Cat will eat me. Here it comes!

As Cat walks onstage, Mouse hurries offstage, squeaking.

LITTLE RED ANT: Cat must be the strongest. I will ask. Cat, are you the strongest of all?

CAT: No, I am not the strongest.

LITTLE RED ANT: Who is stronger than you?

CAT: Stick is stronger. When Stick hits me, I run away. Here it comes!

As Stick walks onstage, Cat hurries offstage, meowing.

164

LITTLE RED ANT: Stick must be the strongest. I will ask. Stick, are you the strongest of all?

STICK: No, I am not the strongest.

LITTLE RED ANT: Who is stronger than you?

STICK: Fire is stronger. When I am put into Fire, Fire burns me up! Here it comes!

As Fire walks onstage, Stick hurries offstage.

LITTLE RED ANT: Fire must be the strongest. I will ask. Fire, are you the strongest of all?

FIRE: No, I am not the strongest.

LITTLE RED ANT: Who is stronger than you?

FIRE: Water is stronger. When Water is poured on me, it kills me. Here it comes!

As Water walks onstage, Fire hurries offstage.

LITTLE RED ANT: Water must be the strongest. I will ask. Water, are you the strongest of all?

WATER: No, I am not the strongest.

LITTLE RED ANT: Who is stronger than you?

WATER: Deer is stronger. When Deer comes, Deer drinks me. Here it comes!

As Deer walks onstage, Water hurries offstage.

LITTLE RED ANT: Deer must be the strongest. I will ask. Deer, are you the strongest of all?

DEER: No, I am not the strongest.

LITTLE RED ANT: Who is stronger than you?

DEER: Arrow is stronger. When Arrow strikes me, it can kill me. Here it comes!

As Arrow walks onstage, Deer runs offstage with leaping bounds.

LITTLE RED ANT: Arrow must be the strongest. I will ask. Arrow, are you the strongest of all?

ARROW: No, I am not the strongest.

LITTLE RED ANT: Who is stronger than you?

ARROW: Big Rock is stronger. When I am shot from the bow and I hit Big Rock, Big Rock breaks me.

LITTLE RED ANT: Do you mean the same Big Rock where the Red Ants live?

ARROW: Yes, that is Big Rock. Here it comes!

As Big Rock walks onstage, Arrow runs offstage.

LITTLE RED ANT: Big Rock must be the strongest. I will ask. Big Rock, are you the strongest of all?

BIG ROCK: No, I am not the strongest.

LITTLE RED ANT: Who is stronger than you?

BIG ROCK: You are stronger. Every day you and the other Red Ants come and carry little pieces of me away. Someday I will be all gone.

Scene III: The Ants' Hole

NARRATOR: So Little Red Ant went back home and spoke to the ant people.

The ants crouch together on the darkened stage.

SECOND ANT: Little Red Ant has returned.

THIRD ANT: He has come back alive!

FOURTH ANT: Tell us about what you have learned. Who is the strongest of all?

LITTLE RED ANT: I have learned that everything is stronger than something else. And even though we ants are small, in some ways *we* are the strongest of all.

STRATEGY SKILL

Summarize
What has Little Red Ant discovered about who is strongest?

WHO'S STRONGER THAN JOE AND LUCIA?

AUTHOR

JOSEPH BRUCHAC was raised in the Adirondack Mountains by his Native American grandparents. As a child, Joseph wanted to share stories about his heritage. When he grew up, he began to write the traditional tales of his people. One day when Joseph was reading one of his books to an audience, he began to tell the tale from memory, just as Native American storytellers did a long time ago. Now Joseph writes and tells his tales.

Other books by Joseph Bruchac: *The Earth Under Sky Bear's Feet* and *The First Strawberries*

ILLUSTRATOR

LUCIA ANGELA PEREZ was introduced to art at an early age. Her mother was a painter and had a pottery business. Lucia became a book illustrator when she finished a book that her mother began. Lucia has been working as an illustrator ever since. She now lives with her family in Texas.

LOG ON Find out more about Joseph Bruchac and Lucia Angela Perez at **www.macmillanmh.com**

Write About It

Little Red Ant went in search of an answer to his question. Describe a time when you had to search to find the answer to a difficult question.

Comprehension Check

Summarize

Use your Story Map to help you summarize *The Strongest One.* Include only the most important information about the play in your summary.

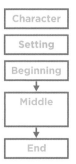

Character
Setting
Beginning
Middle
End

Think and Compare

1. What is the most important thing the different characters tell Little Red Ant? **Generate Questions: Summarize**

2. What did Little Red Ant learn at the end of the play? Use story details to explain how he could feel strong and weak at the same time. **Synthesize**

3. Can you identify something *bigger* but *weaker* than you? Can you identify something *smaller* but *stronger* than you? Explain. **Apply**

4. Little Red Ant learns a lesson about being the strongest. Why is this an important lesson for people to learn? Explain. **Evaluate**

5. Read "The Wind and the Sun" on pages 154–155. Describe the different ways Wind and Sun and Little Red Ant tried to solve their problems. **Reading/Writing Across Texts**

Behind the Scenes at a Play

by Candice Bertoline

The theater goes dark. The **audience** quiets down. The curtain opens. Actors step onto the stage, and the audience sits and waits for the play to begin.

Many people are needed to put on a play. It may take them months to prepare for a performance. Some of these people have made the setting, or **set**, that decorates the stage, and **costumes** for the actors to wear. Actors have auditioned, or tried out, for the parts. Then they have taken time to learn their lines. Even after the play is ready to be performed, the work doesn't end. A lot goes on that the audience does not see. Let's take a peek behind the scenes.

Stagehands change sets quickly and quietly during a performance.

To get ready for the play, actors put on costumes and makeup. These items will help the audience get to know the characters that the actors will play on the stage. Someone backstage may help with costume changes and repairs.

Stage Makeup

Photos with Captions

Photos help you better understand information in the text. Captions explain the photos.

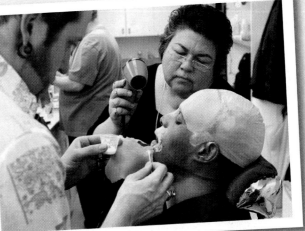

Character makeup changes the way an actor looks.

Straight makeup helps the audience see an actor's face clearly from a distance.

173

Behind the stage, someone keeps track of props that are used on the set. Tables, chairs, and other big things are called set props. Hand props are things the actors can hold. These include phones, cups, and books.

A set is like a costume for the stage. It can look like a forest or a playground or anyplace else you can imagine. Sets may be made from wood, paper, and even fabric. They are usually light so they are easy to move on and off the stage.

The lights in a play are very important. Lighting shows the time of day. It can also set the feeling of a scene. For example, brightness may make the audience feel happy and get their attention. A lighting technician controls the lighting during the play. The technician often sits in a booth at the back of the theater.

This is just some of what's needed to put on a play. Next time you see a performance, imagine all of the people who worked hard to help the performers put on a good show.

Connect and Compare

1. Look at the photos and read the captions about stage makeup on page 173. Why would an actor use character makeup? **Photos with Captions**

2. If you put on a play that took place in a spooky forest, how would you create the right mood onstage? **Apply**

3. Think about this article and *The Strongest One*. Which characters might have special lighting when they are onstage? Explain. **Reading/Writing Across Texts**

Performing Arts Activity

Find out more about lighting effects and props. Then write a short play that uses them. Perform the play for the class.

 Find out more about plays at **www.macmillanmh.com**

Writing

Organization

The main idea is the most important idea of the paragraph and may be stated at the beginning. The other sentences support the main idea.

I wanted to explain why I think music is important. Here is what I wrote.

I tell my main idea in the first two sentences.

Music Is for Everyone

by Luke J.

Music is important because it's something everyone can enjoy. It doesn't matter where you live or what language you speak. A song sounds the same in India as it does in the United States. Music can make people happy. People dance and sing along to songs they like. Also, music brings people together. Look around at a concert. You see kids, teens, and adults, because they all enjoy music.

Your Turn

Write a paragraph that persuades readers to agree with your opinion. Tell why you do or do not think that movies, plays, music, or art museums are important. Be sure that your main idea is clear and that you give facts and opinions to support the main idea. Use the Writer's Checklist to check your writing.

Writer's Checklist

✓ **Ideas and Content:** Is my message clear?

☑ **Organization:** Does my topic sentence tell my opinion? Did I give supporting reasons?

✓ **Voice:** Does my writing sound like I care about the subject?

✓ **Word Choice:** Do my words tell how I feel?

✓ **Sentence Fluency:** Did I write complete sentences?

✓ **Conventions:** Did I capitalize proper nouns, such as the names of days, months, and places? Did I check my spelling?

WOLVES

Talk About It

Wolves are beautiful, wild creatures. Why do you think that they are not kept as pets?

 Find out more about wolves at **www.macmillanmh.com**

Vocabulary

passion	bothering
admire	dangerous
concentrate	ached
splendid	

Dictionary

Multiple-Meaning Words have more than one meaning. Use a dictionary to find the meanings of *concentrate*.

THE BOY WHO CRIED WOLF

retold by Carole Bartell

There was once a young shepherd who lived in a village. This boy loved looking after his sheep. He did his job with **passion**. The villagers always told him what a good job he was doing. His work was easy to **admire**.

HAVING SOME FUN

One day the boy was bored. His mind wandered. He couldn't **concentrate** on watching the sheep. Then he thought of something wonderful to do. He thought it was a **splendid** idea.

He yelled, "Help! Wolf! A wolf is chasing the sheep!"

The villagers came running.

"Where is it?" one man asked.

"There's no wolf," the boy laughed. "I was just having fun."

"We are all busy working. You shouldn't be **bothering** us when there's no wolf!" he said.

Far away, a wolf looked at his watch and waited. He chuckled at his plot to fool the boy and the villagers.

THE NEXT DAY

The next day the boy was bored again. "Wolf!" he cried.

Once again the villagers ran up the hill but saw no wolf.

"Wolves are **dangerous**! They can harm you and the sheep!" they shouted angrily.

ONE DAY LATER

The next day the boy saw the wolf. He cried out, "Wolf! Wolf!"

"Time to run," said the wolf as he chased the sheep.

The villagers didn't come. When they saw the boy next, he was crying. His throat **ached** from crying for help.

"Why didn't you come when I called?" he asked. "A wolf chased all the sheep away."

"No one believes a liar, even if he is telling the truth," they said.

Reread for **Comprehension**

Generate Questions
Fantasy and Reality

Generating, or asking, questions as you read can help you understand the story. Some stories include fantasy—things that could not happen in real life. As you read, ask yourself which things can really happen and which can not.

Reread "The Boy Who Cried Wolf." Use your Fantasy and Reality Chart to help you determine what is fantasy and what is reality.

Fantasy	Reality

Comprehension

Genre

A **Fantasy** is a story with characters, settings, or other elements that could not exist in real life.

Generate Questions

Fantasy and Reality

As you read, use your Fantasy and Reality Chart.

Fantasy	Reality

Read to Find Out

Why does the wolf go to school?

WOLF!

by Becky Bloom
illustrated by Pascal Biet

Award Winning Selection

After walking for many days, a wolf wandered into a quiet little town. He was tired and hungry, his feet **ached**, and he had only a little money that he kept for emergencies.

Then he remembered. There's a farm outside this village, he thought. I'll find some food there . . . .

Fantasy and Reality
Does the wolf act like a real wolf? How can you tell?

185

As he peered over the farm fence, he saw a pig, a duck, and a cow reading in the sun.

The wolf had never seen animals read before. "I'm so hungry that my eyes are playing tricks on me," he said to himself. But he really was very hungry and didn't stop to think about it for long.

The wolf stood up tall, took a deep breath …
and leaped at the animals with a howl—

"AaaOOOOOooo!"

Chickens and rabbits ran for their lives, but the duck,
the pig, and the cow didn't budge.

"What is that awful noise?" complained the cow. "I
can't **concentrate** on my book."

"Just ignore it," said the duck.

Feeling quite satisfied, the wolf went back to the farm and jumped over the fence. I'll show them, he thought.

He opened his book and began to read:

"Run, wolf! Run!

See wolf run."

"You've got a long way to go," said the duck, without even **bothering** to look up. And the pig, the duck, and the cow went on reading their own books, not the least impressed.

The wolf jumped back over the fence and ran straight to the public library. He studied long and hard, reading lots of dusty old books, and he practiced and practiced until he could read without stopping.

"They'll be impressed with my reading now," he said to himself.

The wolf walked up to the farm gate and knocked. He opened *The Three Little Pigs* and began to read:

"Onceuponatimetherewerethreelittlepigsonedaytheir mothercalledthemandtoldthem—"

"Stop that racket," interrupted the duck.

"You have improved," remarked the pig, "but you still need to work on your style."

The wolf tucked his tail between his legs and slunk away.

197

But the wolf wasn't about to give up. He counted the little money he had left, went to the bookshop, and bought a **splendid** new storybook. His first very own book!

He was going to read it day and night, every letter and every line. He would read so well that the farm animals would **admire** him.

Ding-dong, rang the wolf at the farm gate.

He lay down on the grass, made himself comfortable, took out his new book, and began to read.

He read with confidence and **passion**, and the pig, the cow, and the duck all listened and said not one word.

Each time he finished a story, the pig, the duck, and the cow asked if he would please read them another.

So the wolf read on, story after story.

One minute he was Little Red Riding Hood,

the next a genie emerging from a lamp,

and then a swashbuckling pirate.

"This is so much fun!" said the duck.

"He's a master," said the pig.

"Why don't you join us on our picnic today?" offered the cow.

And so they all had a picnic—the pig, the duck, the cow, and the wolf. They lay in the tall grass and told stories all the afternoon long.

"We should all become storytellers," said the cow suddenly.

"We could travel around the world," added the duck.

"We can start tomorrow morning," said the pig.

The wolf stretched in the grass. He was happy to have such wonderful friends.

Read Along with Becky and Pascal

Author
Becky Bloom was born in Greece but has traveled to many countries to work and go to school. She studied architecture at the University of California at Berkeley and now lives in the south of France with her husband and children. She has many different animals around her home, but no wolf.

Other books by Becky Bloom and Pascal Biet: *Leo and Lester* and *Mice Make Trouble*

Illustrator
Pascal Biet has lived in France his whole life. He was born in Saint-Laurent, in the north of France. He studied visual communication and design in Blois, France, and now he lives in Paris.

LOG ON Find out more about Becky Bloom and Pascal Biet at **www.macmillanmh.com**

Write About It

After the wolf learned to read, he felt confident and was able to make friends. What have you learned to do that made you feel really good about yourself?

204

Comprehension Check

Summarize

Use your Fantasy and Reality Chart to help you summarize *Wolf!* Use details from the story to clarify what is fantasy and reality.

Fantasy	Reality

Think and Compare

1. What changes would you suggest to make the story more realistic? **Generate Questions: Fantasy and Reality**

2. What information supports the idea that the wolf wanted to make friends? Use story details in your answer. **Synthesize**

3. Why would you **admire** the wolf if he was able to read you a story? **Apply**

4. Why did the animals like the wolf after he learned to read well? Explain your answer. **Analyze**

5. Read "The Boy Who Cried Wolf" on pages 180-181. Compare it to *Wolf!* In which story do the animal characters act more like real people? Use details from both selections in your answer. **Reading/Writing Across Texts**

Science

Genre

Nonfiction Articles give information about real people, places, or things.

Text Features

Italics, headings, pronunciations, and **bold** or colored type help you understand important information in the text.

Content Vocabulary

reputation   den

offspring   communicate

The Truth About WOLVES

by Paul Netcher

For years wolves have been feared and misunderstood. They are the villains in many folktales. How did these furry animals get such a bad **reputation**? It's because people think they're sneaky and always hunting for food.

The wolf's bad reputation is not truly deserved. It's time to set the record straight. Here is the truth about *Canis lupus*—the gray wolf.

Life in a Pack

Wolves do not like to live near humans. They prefer the company of other wolves. They live in groups called packs. A pack is made up of two parents and their newest **offspring**, or young. Sometimes other wolves become part of a pack, too.

Most packs have six to eight wolves. Some packs can have as many as 30 members!

Wolves often help each other. They live, hunt, and raise pups together. In fact, members of a pack always work together to hunt deer or moose.

Follow the Leader

heading

Using Text Features

These text features help you make sense of what you read.

boldface type

pronunciation

The wolves in a pack have a **hierarchy** (HIGH•er•ar•kee), or order. The pack leaders are called the *alpha* male and female. Each of the other wolves has a role or job within the pack.

italics

Raising the Pups

Pups are born in a well-hidden cave or dirt hole called a **den**. At first, the mother stays with the pups. She lets other members of the pack bring her food. After a few weeks, the mother goes off with the rest of the pack to hunt. Another adult may "babysit" the pups while she is gone. When the pack returns, they chew and spit up meat for the pups.

Young wolves learn how to hunt by playing. They also learn by watching other pack members.

Talking Like a Wolf

Wolves **communicate**, or give information to each other in different ways. Sometimes they use body movements to let other wolves know how they feel. Different howls also have different meanings. One howl calls the pack together. Another howl warns other packs to stay away. Even though many pictures show wolves howling during a full moon, wolves never howl at the moon! They are just communicating with the pack.

Connect and Compare

1. Look at the words "Talking Like a Wolf" on this page. Why are these words in a different size and color? What do we call this text feature? **Using Text Features**

2. What is your opinion of wolves after reading this article? **Evaluate**

3. Use information in this article to tell how the main character in *Wolf!* is different from a real wolf. **Reading/Writing Across Texts**

Science Activity

Do more research about wolves. On the computer, write an article for younger students that tells what you learned. Use text features such as *italics*, *headings*, and *bold* or *colored type* to highlight important parts of your article.

 Find out more about wolves at **www.macmillanmh.com**

Write a Wildlife Protection Poster

Writing

Word Choice

Use specific nouns that identify a particular person, place, thing, or idea. For example, the noun *habitat* gives more specific information than the noun *place*.

I wrote a poster telling why it's important to *save* the *sea turtles*.

I used specific nouns.

Save the Sea Turtles!

by Nate W.

After millions of years sea turtles are becoming extinct. You can help! Throw away ribbons, balloons, plastic bags, and fishing lines. They can harm a turtle's habitat. Don't shine house or car lights onto the beach. Confused turtles follow the lights instead of heading to the sea. Talk to a conservation expert about how else you can help.

Your Turn

Write a paragraph for a poster that persuades people to protect wildlife. It might encourage people to protect a certain animal or to take care of an area in which a certain animal lives. Be sure to use specific nouns in your poster. Use the Writer's Checklist to check your writing.

Writer's Checklist

☑ **Ideas and Content:** Do I provide information to explain my message?

☑ **Organization:** Did I get the reader's attention at the beginning of the poster?

☑ **Voice:** Did I show that I have strong feelings?

☐ **Word Choice:** Did I use specific nouns?

☑ **Sentence Fluency:** Does my writing sound good when I read it out loud?

☑ **Conventions:** Did I write complete sentences and use end marks? Did I form plural nouns correctly? Did I check my spelling?

211

Talk About It

What do you think the world and your life will be like in the future?

LOG ON Find out more about the future at **www.macmillanmh.com**

212

Past, Present, and Future

Where Did the First Americans Live ?

Vocabulary

- **objects**
- **entertainment**
- **predictions**
- **computers**

Did the first Americans paint these images?

Bering Land Bridge

Atlantic Ocean

Cave of the Painted Rock

Pacific Ocean

BRAZIL

This yellow line shows the way the first Americans might have traveled into South America.

An ancient campsite has been discovered in a cave in Brazil. Archaeologists, who study ancient people, call it the Cave of the Painted Rock. Paintings on the cave walls are clues that people lived here 11,000 years ago. They were probably the first Americans.

An Important Discovery

Archaeologist Anna Roosevelt and other scientists began exploring the Cave of the Painted Rock in 1990. The team found paintings of stick figures and animals, handprints, fish bones, and tools. They also found charred wood, palm seeds, and other **objects**. These show that people cooked, ate, and worked in the cave.

Early Americans used minerals to finger-paint on the rock walls. This was probably for **entertainment**. It seems that they had an artistic, fun side.

Tracing Their Steps

Many scientists believe the first people to reach America came from Asia. They crossed a land bridge that once connected the areas that are now Russia and Alaska.

Predictions for the Present

What did people long ago think life would be like today? Here's what some experts in the past said about the world we live in right now. How many of their predictions were right?

"Everything that can be invented has been invented." –Charles Duell, head of the U.S. Patent Office, 1899

"The radio craze . . . will die out in time." –Thomas Edison, 1922

"I think there is a world market for about five **computers**." –Thomas Watson, chairman of IBM, 1943

"There is no reason for any individual to have a computer in their home." –Ken Olson, president of Digital Equipment Corporation, 1977

What a Century It Was!

From 1900 to 1999, the world went through some major changes. We flew in airplanes. We went into space in rockets and shuttles. Computers were hooked up in homes and schools across the country. People fought for freedom and equality. The list goes on and on. Here are a few of the inventions and discoveries of the incredible twentieth century.

1904 Ice cream cone
1907 Plastic
1926 Movies with sound
1927 Television
1939 Jet airplane
1969 Early Internet
1972 Handheld calculator
1973 Cellular phone
1981 Space shuttle
1993 Web browser for exploring the Internet
1997 Pathfinder explores Mars

LOG ON   Find out more about the twentieth century at **www.macmillanmh.com**

215

What's in Store for the Future?

Comprehension

Genre

Nonfiction Articles give information about real people, places, or things.

Summarize

Fact and Opinion

A fact is something that can be proven to be true. An opinion is a belief that may not be supported by facts.

How can new knowledge and inventions improve our daily lives in the future?

217

Modern inventions make our everyday lives easier, but many of these inventions use up natural resources. Cars burn gas to get us where we want to go. This pollutes the air. Electric heat and light make our homes warm and welcoming, but they also burn up coal and oil. We need factories, but factory waste pollutes our waterways.

Experts believe that changing the way we live in the future may actually improve our planet's health. We can use cleaner energy and fewer chemicals as we build the towns of tomorrow. Here are some ideas and **predictions** that many people think will make our planet a cleaner place to live.

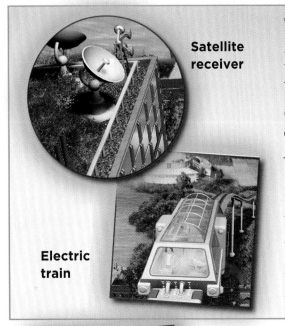

Satellite receiver

Electric train

Work and Transportation

More and more people will be working in their homes using **computers** and satellite receivers. Today, more electric trains are being built, and new hydrogen-powered and electric cars are being developed. In the future, most cars will probably use this technology. Shopping and **entertainment** may be as close as a ride on an Earth-friendly bicycle.

Organic farm

Home garden

Food

We'll grow fruits, grains, and vegetables close to home, either in our gardens or on nearby organic farms. The farms won't use chemicals to control pests. Instead, different kinds of insects will stop harmful bugs. That will help keep chemicals out of our food.

Shopping

Mall

Online stores will be popular, but we'll still have malls. They will be small, with bike racks instead of a giant parking lot. They will use natural sunlight to cut down on energy use. They will also recycle the **objects** you buy there, when you are finished using them.

Energy

Energy from windmills and solar panels is available now to some homeowners. In the future, every home will probably use this kind of energy. Rooftop solar panels will help make hydrogen from sunlight. Our appliances will run on this gas. At night hydrogen will be turned into electricity or light.

Windmills

Waste

Plumbing lines will empty into enclosed marshes, where special plants, fish, snails, and bacteria will clean wastewater. Clean water will flow back into streams and reservoirs.

Enclosed marsh

Think and Compare

STRATEGY SKILL

1. Which statements in this article are fact, and which are opinion? Explain your answer.

2. What problems do gas-powered cars create?

3. Which one of these predictions do you think would affect you the most? Why?

4. The "Predictions for the Present" did not come true. Which predictions in "What's in Store for the Future?" do you think will come true, and which won't come true? Give reasons for your answers.

WILL ROBOTS DO ALL THE WORK?

Do homework, chores, and the long school day make you wish you had more time to just "kid" around? That wish may come true for your grandchildren. Scientists are inventing things to make life easier and more fun in the year 2050.

By 2050, robots may be in every room in the home. Professor Eric Schwartz of the University of Florida predicts, "A robot could clean the child's room and play catch." Schwartz's team has already created a robot that vacuums and is now developing one that mows the lawn.

By 2050, kids will be able to call friends on a videophone, says Texas Instruments' Gene Frantz. They will surf the Internet, watch TV, and type up homework by talking into a wristwatch-sized gadget. People who are sick will wear electronic chips that deliver medicine to the bloodstream.

Marcia Kuszmaul of Microsoft Education Group says small computers will allow kids in the future to "learn any time, any place." Instead of textbooks, students will use an electronic reader that delivers their assignments.

Go On ▶

Directions: Answer the questions.

1. **How can computers give you more time for fun?**

   A   Computers will cost less in the future.
   B   All learning will take place over a videophone.
   C   All kids will have robots that will go to school for them.
   D   They help you do chores and homework more quickly.

2. **According to the author, in the future**

   A   kids will learn in school and at home.
   B   teachers will not be necessary.
   C   kids will not learn to read.
   D   only grandchildren will have computers.

3. **This article is MOSTLY about**

   A   grandchildren of the future.
   B   technology changing our lives.
   C   how hard life is for kids today.
   D   robots for kids.

4. **What kinds of jobs do you think robots are suited to do? Why?**

5. **Explain how you think changes to computers will change your daily life in the future.**

> **Tip**
> You have to think about the entire passage to choose the best answer.

Write to a Prompt

What if you could borrow the vacuuming robot for a day? Write a diary entry about this experience. Describe what happened and how you felt about it.

My topic sentence tells you what I am writing about.

A Day with Robot Bob

My amazing day began when Professor Schwartz brought his robot, Bob, to my house. I was surprised that Bob didn't look like a person at all. He was just a small machine with wheels, but what a neat machine!

I learned how to program Bob to turn and to go forward and backward. In a way, Bob worked like a remote-controlled car. The difference was he vacuumed while he rolled along.

A robot doesn't really do all the work for you. I had to pick up everything from the floor of my room. Then Bob was able to work. He doesn't really think for himself either. I had to tell him how to move. It was still a lot of work, but it was fun to run a machine without having to touch it.

Professor Schwartz and his team are working to make Bob "smarter." Then he won't need so much help "learning" about what he has to do. I hope I see him again someday.

222

Writing Prompt

Think back to an experience you had using something new like a toy or computer. Write a diary entry about what happened and how you felt trying something for the first time. Be sure to choose your topic carefully, and include details in your story.

Writer's Checklist

- ☑ Ask yourself, who will read my story?
- ☑ Think about your purpose for writing.
- ☑ Plan your writing before beginning.
- ☑ Use details to support your story.
- ☑ Be sure your story has a beginning, a middle, and an ending.
- ☑ Use your best spelling, grammar, and punctuation.

OUT IN SPACE

Talk About It

What do you think about when you look into the sky at night?

LOG ON Find out more about the night sky at **www.macmillanmh.com**

The constellation Orion

Constellations: Pictures in the Sky

by Tyler Giliberto

Looking up at the night sky, you won't see the sun and all nine planets that belong to our **solar system**, but you can enjoy the light of the moon and the surrounding stars. Long ago, people tried to make sense of the stars that fill the night sky. They saw that the stars made patterns in the sky that looked like people, animals, and other things. These groups of stars were called constellations. Today there are 88 constellations in the sky.

Ursa Major

Ursa Major or "Great Bear" is **easily** one of the best-known constellations. Some Native American legends say that "the giant bear has three warriors chasing it." Inside Ursa Major, you can find the Big Dipper. The Big Dipper is a group of stars that looks like a cup with a long handle.

Orion: The Great Hunter

Orion is another constellation. In a famous Greek myth, Orion was a great hunter. He was killed when he stepped on a scorpion. The Greek gods felt sorry for him. They put him and his dogs in the sky as constellations. Then they put all the animals he hunted near him. They placed the scorpion **farther** away so Orion wouldn't be hurt by it again.

226

The **main** star of this constellation marks Orion's left shoulder and is called Betelgeuse [BEE-t'l-juhs]. Next to the brightness of this star, all the others appear **dim**.

How bright stars appear depend on their distance from Earth, how large they are, and their different **temperatures**, or how hot they burn. Scientists can use a powerful **telescope** to observe the stars closely and find out more about them.

Scientists know that Betelgeuse is 630 times larger than our sun and shines 60,000 times brighter. It is one of the largest stars anywhere in the night sky, and **probably** one of the most fascinating to study.

An illustration of Orion

Reread for **Comprehension**

STRATEGY SKILL

Generate Questions
Summarize

As you generate or ask questions to summarize an article, think about the important details. To determine which details are important, ask "Do these details support the main idea of the passage?"

Main Idea	Details

A Main Idea Chart helps you decide which information is important enough to include in a summary. Reread the selection to summarize the main ideas and important details.

227

Comprehension

Genre

Informational Nonfiction uses facts to explain about real people, things, places, situations, or events.

Generate Questions

Summarize

As you read, use your Main Idea Chart.

Main Idea	Details

Read to Find Out

What do you need to see other planets in the night sky?

The Planets in Our Solar System

Award Winning Author

by Franklyn M. Branley
illustrated by Kevin O'Malley

229

We all live on a planet. Our planet is called Earth.
It is one of nine planets that go around the sun.

MERCURY

VENUS

EARTH

MARS

JUPITER

SATURN

URANUS

NEPTUNE

PLUTO

You **probably** know the names of some of the planets. Maybe you know all of them. The nine planets are Mercury, Venus, Earth, Mars, Jupiter, Saturn, Uranus, Neptune, and Pluto.

The nine planets are part of the **solar system**.

The most important part of the solar system is the sun. The word *sol* means sun in Latin. So the solar system means "the sun system."

After the sun, the most important parts of the solar system are the nine planets.

Summarize
What are the two most important parts of the solar system?

Have you ever tried to find the planets in the sky? Uranus, Neptune, and Pluto are very **dim**. You need a **telescope** to see them.

You don't need a telescope to see Venus, Mars, Jupiter, or Saturn. They look like bright stars, but they don't twinkle. They glow. You may have seen them and thought they were stars.

You don't need a telescope to see Mercury, either. You can see it in early evening just after sunset. The sky is not very dark then, so you have to be a good sky watcher to find Mercury.

But there is another part of the solar system that you can see **easily**. It is the moon. The moon goes around Earth. It's called Earth's satellite. Most of the other planets also have satellites.

STRATEGY SKILL

Summarize
What objects in the sky can you see without a telescope?

Asteroids are also part of the solar system. So are comets and meteoroids. Asteroids are big chunks of rock that go around the sun. Many are as big as a house. Some are as big as a mountain, or even bigger.

Comets are collections of ice, gas, and dust. The center of a comet may be only a few miles across. The tail of gasses may be millions of miles long.

Meteoroids are bits of rock and metal. Some are as large as boulders, but most are as small as grains of sand. Have you ever seen a shooting star? It was not really a star. It was a meteoroid falling toward Earth.

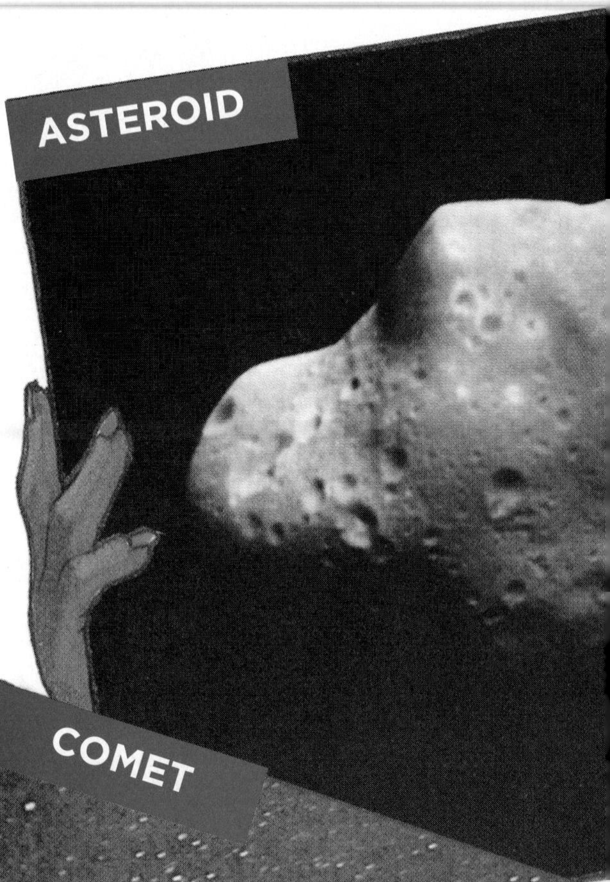

ASTEROID

COMET

The Hale-Bopp Comet could be seen for several months in the spring of 1997.

Asteroid 243 Ida was photographed by the Galileo spacecraft in 1993. It appears to be 32 miles long.

METEORITE

This Mars meteorite was found in the ice fields of Antarctica and is 4.5 billion years old.

237

The solar system has many parts—the sun, the nine planets, the satellites of the planets, asteroids, comets, and meteoroids. The **main** parts are the sun and nine planets.

Seven of the planets have one or more satellites. Four of them have rings.

The nine planets move around the sun. They move in paths called orbits. The drawing shows the orbits.

Mercury takes only 88 days to go around the sun.

Pluto takes much longer than that. It takes about 248 years.

URANUS

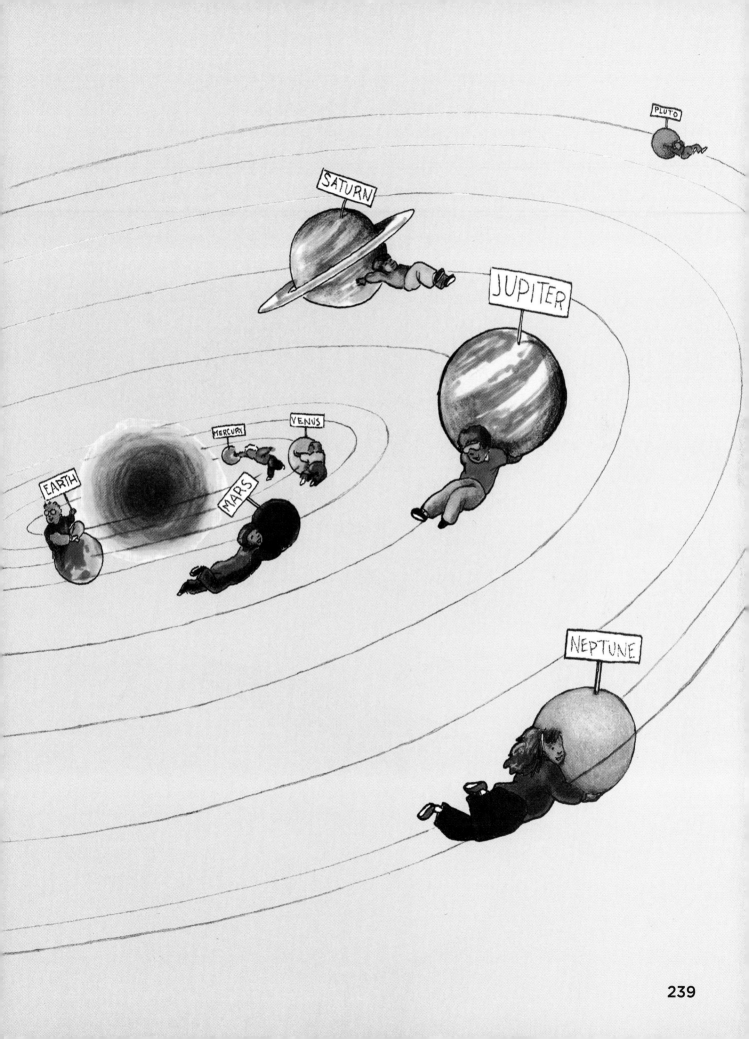

Mercury is closer to the sun than any other planet, but even Mercury is millions of miles from the sun.

Suppose you could fly from Mercury to the sun in a rocket. And suppose the rocket went 50,000 miles an hour. It would take more than four weeks to get there.

Pluto's Orbit

1999

SUN

Neptune's Orbit

1979

It would take the same rocket over eight years to go from Pluto to the sun.

Pluto is usually **farther** from the sun than any other planet. From 1979 to 1999, it was closer to the sun than Neptune. In 1999, Pluto once again became the farthest planet from the sun. It will stay that way until 2250.

Neptune and Pluto are farthest from the sun. That is why they are the coldest planets. **Temperatures** on these planets are about 328°F below zero.

That's much colder than any place on Earth. Even the South Pole never gets that cold.

Mercury and Venus are the hottest planets. The temperature on Mercury reaches 600°F. Sometimes it is much colder. On Venus the temperature stays around 860°F.

Plants and animals cannot live on Mercury or Venus. They would burn up. They cannot live on Neptune or Pluto either. They would freeze. Jupiter and Saturn are also very cold.

Of all the planets, Earth is the only one where people live. We think no other planet in our solar system has plants or animals of any kind. Earth is the "life planet."

Earth is a middle-sized planet. Four of the planets are smaller than Earth. They are Mercury, Venus, Mars, and Pluto. Four of the planets are larger than Earth. They are Jupiter, Saturn, Uranus, and Neptune.

Jupiter is the biggest of all the planets.

It is much bigger than Earth. Suppose Jupiter were a large, hollow ball. Over 1,000 Earths could fit inside it.

Pluto is the smallest planet. It is much smaller than Earth. It is even smaller than the moon. More than 100,000 Plutos would fit inside Jupiter.

Earth is the most important planet to you, and to all of us. That's because it's the planet where we live. It is not the biggest planet in the solar system, nor is it the smallest. It is not the hottest or the coldest. Earth is about in the middle. And it's just right for us.

Franklyn and Kevin Are Out of This World!

Author

Franklyn M. Branley was an astronomer and a chairman of the American Museum of Natural History's Hayden Planetarium. When he was not studying the solar system, he spent a lot of time writing books. He wrote more than 150 of them for children!

Other books by Franklyn M. Branley: *The Sky Is Full of Stars* and *What the Moon Is Like.*

Illustrator

Kevin O'Malley loves to visit classrooms to talk about his books almost as much as he loves to illustrate them. Kevin has also written and illustrated his own books, including *Carl Caught a Flying Fish.*

LOG ON Find out more about Franklyn M. Branley and Kevin O'Malley at **www.macmillanmh.com**

Write About It

The solar system is filled with amazing sights. If you could take a trip into space, what would you want to see close-up? Explain.

Comprehension Check

Summarize

Use your Main Idea Chart to summarize the parts of our solar system as described in *The Planets in Our Solar System*. Summarize the main idea and tell the most important details.

Main Idea	Details

Think and Compare

1. How would you summarize the explanation of Pluto's distance from the sun? **Generate Questions: Summarize**

2. Reread pages 234-235. How would you look for planets in the night sky? Use details from the selection to support your answer. **Apply**

3. Why is the sun described as the most important part of the **solar system**? **Analyze**

4. Describe why you believe that Earth is the most important planet to us. **Evaluate**

5. Reread "Constellations: Pictures in the Sky" on pages 226–227. How do the stars in the night sky compare to the planets? Use details from both selections in your answer. **Reading/Writing Across Texts**

Genre

Nonfiction Articles give information about real people, places, or things.

Text Feature

SKILL

Internet Articles provide information online.

Content Vocabulary

URL	hyperlinks
sidebar	home page
menu	

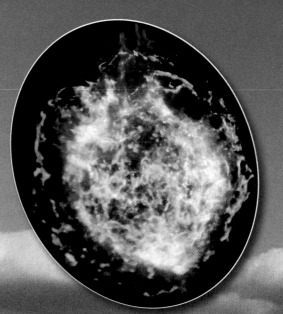

Chandra's photo of the remains of an exploded star

STAR RESEARCH

BY ALYSSA S.

I have read about stars and wanted to find out more about how scientists observe them. My teacher suggested I do research on the Internet. First, I typed in the **URL** that my teacher gave me. I put it in the address line at the top of the page.

A URL is an address for where you want to go on the Internet. Each URL takes you to a Web site with one or more Web pages.

An article on the site talked about Chandra and Hubble. I used the **sidebar**, which is a column at the side of the Web page that has more information. I found out that these are large telescopes out in space.

I saw a **menu** of **hyperlinks** on the side of the page. The menu lists all the articles and information that are on the Web site. You can click on a hyperlink to take you to another page with more information. I clicked on the word *X-ray* to learn what it means. Hyperlinks can be underlined, or in boldface. Some photos are also hyperlinks that take you to a larger image.

Next, I clicked on the hyperlink for the **home page**. The home page usually has a site map. A site map is like the table of contents in a book. It tells you what's on the site. On the home page, I found links to more cool articles about stars. Some even had sound and video. Internet articles made it so easy for me to find out all about stars!

Internet articles, like the one below, provide information online. More information can be found by using the menu, sidebar, and hyperlinks.

URL **home page** **hyperlink** **sidebar** **menu**

Space Searchers 01/12/06

http://www.example.com/

Space Searchers

Home Page

Words to Know

NASA
Observatory
Telescope

More About

Hubble
Chandra
Keck

SEEING INTO SPACE

January 12, 2006

The National Aeronautics and Space Administration (NASA) uses different kinds of observatories (OB·ZER·VA·TOR·EES) to observe, or look at, objects in space. Some of NASA's observatories are telescopes that orbit or float in space around Earth. Other large telescopes are built on the ground.

NASA launched the Hubble Space Telescope in 1990. Shuttle astronauts visit the telescope about every three years to replace and fix parts of Hubble. Every day, Hubble gathers enough information to fill a typical home computer.

The Chandra X-ray Observatory was launched into space on July 23, 1999. It is the newest of NASA's observatories. Chandra's X-ray telescope can see objects that are billions of light-years away.

The Chandra Observatory

The W. M. Keck Observatory in Hawaii uses two telescopes. Each is about eight stories tall. Scientists switch between the two telescopes every one to five days.

A photo from the Keck Observatory

X-ray Telescopes

X-ray telescopes let scientists see extremely hot objects in space. They record X-rays that shine from space objects like a camera taking a picture. Sometimes things come between the object that is shining X-ray light and the telescope. Then the telescope can take a picture of that middle object. It looks like a shadow, the same way an X-ray of your arm might look at the doctor's office.

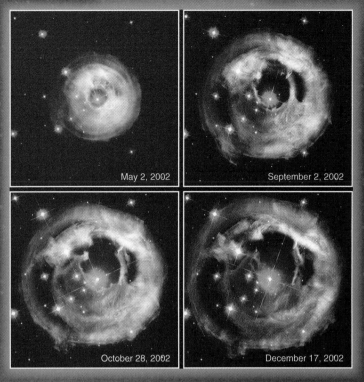

May 2, 2002

September 2, 2002

October 28, 2002

December 17, 2002

Pictures taken by the Hubble telescope

Connect and Compare

1. Look at the Internet article on page 252. Where would you click to learn more about Hubble? **Reading Internet Articles**

2. Compare an Internet article with an article from a textbook or magazine. How are they the same? How are they different? **Analyze**

3. Pretend that page 239 from *The Planets in Our Solar System* is part of an Internet article. Which words could be used as hyperlinks to more information? **Reading/Writing Across Texts**

Science Activity

With an adult, research another observatory on the Internet. Write a paragraph telling what you found.

 Find out more about stars at **www.macmillanmh.com**

Writing

Voice

Writers show excitement by using powerful words that show how they feel. For example, if you like something, you may say it's *good*, but if you love something, you may say it's *terrific* or *amazing*.

I wanted the kids in my class to visit the planetarium. This is the radio ad I wrote.

I used words that show excitement.

Come See the Sky Dome

by Alicia M.

Do you want to have a real space adventure? Then hurry over to the new *Sky Dome* at Bock Planetarium. It's out of this world! You can see planets, moons, stars, and constellations up close. It's like you are in a huge spaceship! And don't forget your umbrella. There are meteor showers, too. The planetarium is open seven days a week. It will give you a big thrill. Don't miss it!

Your Turn

Write a radio ad for a planetarium or a museum. You may focus on a special attraction, show, or exhibit. Be sure to use words that show excitement in your ad. Use the Writer's Checklist to check your writing.

Writer's Checklist

✓ **Ideas and Content:** Is my message clear?

✓ **Organization:** Is the information well-organized?

 Voice: Does it sound like I care about my message?

✓ **Word Choice:** Did I use persuasive words?

✓ **Sentence Fluency:** Are my sentences easy to read aloud?

✓ **Conventions:** Did I use apostrophes properly in possessive nouns? Did I check my spelling?

Being a Writer

Talk About It

Writing can be a lot of fun. What are your favorite kinds of things to write?

LOG ON Find out more about being a writer at **www.macmillanmh.com**

Talking to Lulu Delacre, children's author

by Diana Jarvis

Lulu Delacre has written and illustrated many books, including *Golden Tales* and *The Bossy Gallito.* Some of her books have won awards. I wanted to sit and talk with this successful writer.

Q: What were you like at school? Were you **talented**?

A: I was a good student at school. Yes, I was talented. I could see things in a way that I could transfer them onto paper. I loved to draw and create.

Q: Were books always special to you? What is your **single** favorite book?

A: In my house, books had their own special room—my father's study. I loved being in that room. If I have to choose, my favorite book is *Voyage to the Center of the Earth* by Jules Verne.

Q: Writing is difficult. Is there a **proper**, or correct, way to write?

A: I don't believe there's a proper way to write a book. I keep a journal. I draw in it. I also write ideas and things that I find interesting. I reread these journals. At times, a book is born out of these ideas.

Q: Being a writer must be fun. What is the most **excitement** you have ever had as a writer?

A: It was when *The Bossy Gallito* won the Pura Belpré Honor for text and illustration.

Q: What was the first story you sold to a publisher? Tell us about that **acceptance**.

A: Many years ago I created two characters—an elephant named Nathan and his mouse friend named Nicholas Alexander. Out of the sketches I made of these characters, a story was born. Then it was accepted and published.

Q: What is the most **useful** thing kids can do to help their writing?

A: Read, read, read. And keep a journal to write whatever comes into your mind.

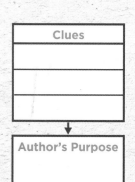

Reread for **Comprehension**

STRATEGY SKILL

Summarize
Author's Purpose
An author writes to entertain, inform, or persuade. As you read, stop and summarize what you have read. Then ask yourself "Why did the author write this information?"

Reread "Talking to Lulu Delacre." As you read, summarize the author's purpose. Use the Author's Purpose Chart to help you.

Clues

↓

Author's Purpose

Comprehension

Genre
An **Autobiography** is the story of a person's life written by that person.

Summarize
Author's Purpose
As you read, use your Author's Purpose Chart.

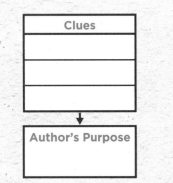

Clues

↓

Author's Purpose

Read to Find Out
Why does the author decide to write children's stories?

260

AUTHOR
A TRUE STORY

written and illustrated by
Helen Lester

Award Winning Selection

A LONG TIME AGO there lived a three-year-old author. Me. I was the best grocery-list writer in the world and a huge help to my mother. When I wrote a word I knew <u>exactly</u> what it said.

And the fun part was that I could turn each list upside down and the words said the same thing. I think I made hundreds of these **useful** lists for my mother, and she never once said, "No thank you, dear, I have enough."

"Then I went to school and learned to make what they called "real letters." My writing was the prettiest in the class, with straight straight lines and round round lines. It was perfect. And it was perfectly backwards.

I didn't just mix up b's and d's. That's easy to do because they look so much alike. My letters started at the right (well, wrong) side of the paper and marched across, pretty as could be—and backwards.

There's a name for somebody with this problem. I was a "mirror writer." My teachers had to hold my work up to a mirror to understand what I had written.

Thanks to a lot of help, I was finally able to write in the **proper** direction. But writing stories was so HARD for me!

Often I couldn't come up with a **single** idea, and my stories got stuck in the middle, and I couldn't think of a title, and I had trouble making the changes my teacher wanted me to make, and I lost my pencils, and I wondered why I was doing this, and I got very very VERY frustrated.

Author's Purpose
Why does the author explain how she used to write as a child?

So I spent a lot of time dreaming about what I wanted to be when I grew up. Since no one from the circus came looking for me, I became a teacher. I learned that teachers do not live in schools, eating only crackers and milk and sleeping under their desks.

I also learned that teaching was fun and that children have fantastic imaginations. So my favorite subject to teach was—writing!

One day a friend said, "You should write a children's book."

And I thought, "I spent ten years in second grade, so I know a child from a chicken. Maybe I should."

I went right home and wrote a book. It was the best book I had ever written. Of course, it was the only book I had ever written.

I illustrated it with my nicest drawings and proudly sent it to a publisher. "Lucky people," I thought.

The lucky people sent it back and said, "No thank you." That's called a rejection. I decided I'd never write again.

Until the next day, when I felt better. I wrote a second book and sent it to a different publisher. The second publisher sent the book back. "No thank you." I decided I'd never write again. Until the next day, when I felt better. I wrote another book.

And another.

And another.

And another.

Practice must have helped each story get a little better, for on my seventh try no book came back. Just a "Yes please." That's called an **acceptance**.

I was beside myself with joy and **excitement**. I was the first author I had ever met.

I drew the pictures for my first book. And I did the pictures for this book. But usually I work with an illustrator who has been to art school and who can draw bicycles and refrigerators and pigs. This **talented** person draws what I would if I could.

So here I am. An author! And every time I sit down to write, perfect words line up in perfect order and WHOOP—a perfect book pops out of the computer.

Well, not exactly. Sometimes writing stories is so HARD for me! I can't come up with a single idea, and my stories get stuck in the middle, and I can't think of a title, and I have trouble making the changes my editor wants me to make, and I lose my pencils, and I wonder why I'm doing this, and I get very very VERY frustrated.

But that's sometimes. I love it best when ideas are hatching so fast I can barely write them down. I grab the nearest thing to write on and get so excited I forget what I was doing in the first place. The ideas that come in the middle of the night are hard to read the next day.

Not all of the ideas are useful. I keep a whole box full of fizzled thoughts and half-finished books. I call it my Fizzle Box. Whenever I need an idea, I can go to the box and find wonderful things

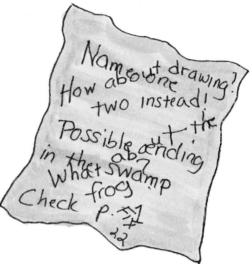

—just the name I needed!

—a funny word!

—a wise lesson!

Author's Purpose
How does the author show that writing can be hard, but it can be fun as well?

269

Usually when I first think a book is finished, it really isn't. I keep going over the story again and again, looking for ways to make it better with little changes here and there. I do this until the book has to be printed. Then it's too late to do anything more!

I used to think that writing had to be done at a special time, while sitting at a desk. But slowly I discovered that I could write <u>any</u>time. And <u>any</u>where. I especially like to write when I'm bored, because then I'm not anymore.

Of course, writing anyTIME anyWHERE sometimes means writing on anyTHING.

Authors are lucky, for they get to meet hundreds of children through letters, school and library visits, and at autographing sessions. I didn't always like autographing books. The first time I autographed, my table was next to the table of a very famous author. I was not a very famous author.

Her line had no end. Mine had no beginning.

I'm glad I didn't join the circus. Even though writing is sometimes hard work, it's what I love to do. I never dreamed I'd become an author. So this is better than a dream come true.

Get Creative
with Helen Lester!

Helen Lester first discovered how much fun writing can be when she was a girl and read her parents' interesting letters. Helen did not think about actually becoming an author until she was a grownup. When she became a mother, Helen read funny books to her children every night. Then she decided to make her own funny books. Helen says that she starts a book whenever a good idea pops into her head. Ideas pop up at really strange times, like when she is at the kitchen sink washing spinach!

Other books by Helen Lester: *Hooway for Wodney Wat* and *Tacky the Penguin*

HOOWAY FOR WODNEY WAT

TACKY the Penguin

LOG ON Find out more about Helen Lester at **www.macmillanmh.com**

Write About It

Helen Lester chose to be a writer. What would you like to be? Why?

Comprehension Check

Summarize

Use the Author's Purpose Chart to help you summarize *Author: A True Story.* In your summary include reasons why the author became a writer.

Clues

↓

Author's Purpose

Think and Compare

1. Why does the author tell us that writing is hard for her? Use your Author's Purpose Chart to explain. **Summarize: Author's Purpose**

2. Why did the author's friend say that she should write children's books? Use story details in your answer. **Analyze**

3. How would you use the ideas and information in this story to become a successful author? **Apply**

4. What might have happened if the author's stories never gained **acceptance** from publishers? Explain. **Synthesize**

5. Read "Talking to Lulu Delacre" on pages 258–259. How do you think the author of *Author: A True Story* would answer each of these interview questions? In what ways might the two authors' experiences be different? **Reading/Writing Across Texts**

Poetry

Poetry uses elements such as rhyme, rhythm, and repetition to express feelings and ideas.

Literary Elements

Alliteration is the repetition of the same beginning sound in a series of words.

Repetition happens when words or phrases are repeated throughout a poem.

Departing and *day* both begin with *d*. This is an example of alliteration.

The phrase "Where I sit writing I can see" is repeated throughout the poem.

Where I Sit Writing

Where I sit writing I can see
A page, a pen, a line or three
Of scribbled verse; a cup of tea.

A spider's web, a windowpane,
A garden blurred a bit with rain,
A low and leaden sky; a plane.

Where I sit writing I can see
An evening sky, a sodden tree,
A windowpane reflecting … me.

Out in the garden's fading light,
Departing day, approaching night,
He copies every word I write.

Where I sit writing I can see
A hand, a pen, a verse or three;
A distant road; a cup—no tea.

A list of rhymes, some crossings out,
Confusions, choices, doodles, doubt.
No clue to what it's all about.

Where I sit writing I can see
A glowing sky, a darkened tree,
Some sticky tape, a saucer … me.

— *Allan Ahlberg*

Poetry

Connect and Compare

SKILL ✓

1. Besides "departing day," what other examples of alliteration can you find in this poem? **Alliteration**

2. Why do you think the author repeats the phrase "Where I sit writing I can see"? **Analyze**

3. In *Author, a True Story*, the author describes some of the frustrations of being a writer. Does the author of this poem express any of the same frustrations? Explain. **Reading/ Writing Across Texts**

LOG ON Find out more about poetry at **www.macmillanmh.com**

275

Writing

Sentence Fluency

Vary the length of your sentences to help your writing flow better. Too many short sentences make your writing choppy. Too many long sentences may make your writing tiring to read.

I wanted to tell about my favorite book. Here is what I wrote.

I used short and long sentences.

Beezus and Ramona

by Alaina M.

My favorite book is <u>Beezus and Ramona</u> by Beverly Cleary. The book is about a nine-year-old girl named Beezus. She has a little sister named Ramona. Beezus tries to look out for her sister, but Ramona is always causing a lot of trouble. The craziest part is when Ramona secretly invites 15 of her four-year-old friends to their house for a party! You will love this book. It is a lot of fun, and it makes you think about how families get along.

Your Turn

Write a review of one of your favorite books. Your review should persuade friends or classmates to read the book. Give the book's title and author. Briefly explain what the book is about and why you like it. Be sure to use both short and long sentences in your review. Use the Writer's Checklist to check your writing.

Writer's Checklist

✓ **Ideas and Content:** Does my book review persuade the reader to read the book?

✓ **Organization:** Did I present details about the book in an order that makes sense?

✓ **Voice:** Did I show how much I like this book?

✓ **Word Choice:** Did I explain my feelings?

 Sentence Fluency: Did I vary the lengths of my sentences?

✓ **Conventions:** Did I capitalize the title and underline it? Did I use *and* to combine sentences?

Venus Flytrap: The Plant with Bite!

by Kim Christopher

Imagine a plant that eats living things. What pops into your mind? Do you picture a huge jungle plant with open jaws or a plant that looks like it came from another planet? Think again! The United States is home to an amazing plant that eats live food, and the plant is not as strange as you might think.

You may have seen or heard of this carnivorous, or meat-eating, plant. It is called the Venus flytrap. It grows in very few places, such as wetlands near the coast of North Carolina and South Carolina.

The Venus flytrap is a carnivorous plant.

278

Go On ▶

The Venus flytrap is not a large plant. It grows to be only about a foot tall. You might walk right past it if you weren't looking for it. The plant has white flowers in the spring, but it is the plant's leaves that make it so interesting. The ends of the leaves have folding parts with stiff, tiny hairs. These are the plant's "traps."

What does the Venus flytrap eat? As you might guess, the Venus flytrap eats flies. It also eats ants, spiders, caterpillars, and crickets. The Venus flytrap makes most of its food with sun, air, and water, just like other plants. Live food just gives it extra nutrition to grow well in damp soil.

Just how does this plant trap and eat living things? The Venus flytrap uses a sweet liquid called nectar to attract its food. Bugs are drawn to the nectar. When one lands on one of the plant's open traps, hairs on the surface make the trap shut. Snap! The trap closes, and the bug is dinner!

The Venus flytrap has small white flowers.

It only takes about a half
second for the trap to close!

The bristles along the edges of the trap lace together so the bug cannot get out. Then the trap digests the bug like a tiny stomach! Each trap lasts for a few meals before another takes its place.

If you want to have your own Venus flytrap at home, you have to buy the plant from a nursery. You can't take a Venus flytrap from where it grows! There are laws about taking it out of the wild.

If you are ever near the coast of North or South Carolina, you might spot a Venus flytrap. Maybe you will even see it bite down on a tasty bug. Yum!

Go On ▶

Tip

Connect the clues from the passage to choose the best answer.

Directions: Answer the questions.

1. **Why would the author write an article about an unusual plant?**

   A   to entertain readers
   B   to give information
   C   to tell you to buy one
   D   to get you to go see where it grows

2. **Why are there laws to stop you from taking plants that grow in the wild?**

   A   to make sure you buy them with money
   B   to keep you from getting hurt
   C   to protect the plants from extinction
   D   to prevent you from getting sick

3. **The author says that Venus flytraps are amazing plants. What word is an antonym, or the opposite, of *amazing*?**

   A   exciting   C   remarkable
   B   confusing   D   boring

4. **How does the Venus flytrap catch and digest its food?**

5. **How is the Venus flytrap different from other plants you have seen? In what ways is it the same? Use details from the selection to support your answer.**

   Writing Prompt
   Some people want to stop laws that protect plants and animals found in the wild. Do you agree? Write a letter to a newspaper explaining how you feel. Include facts to support your ideas.

 281

FOOD AROUND THE WORLD

Talk About It

What was the most interesting food from another culture that you have ever eaten?

LOG ON Find out more about foods from around the world at **www.macmillanmh.com**

Family Feast

by Arthur Stam

It was time for our end-of-year class party, and everyone was having trouble coming up with good ideas, including me.

"How about a carnival with games and cotton candy?" said Penny.

"I know!" said Megan. "A talent show with prizes and pizza!"

"Those are great ideas," said Mr. Ortiz. "What do you think about inviting our families to be **guests** at a foods-of-the-world festival? We can each bring our family's favorite dish. All of that food will make a lovely **banquet**."

The class liked the idea and seemed **agreeable** to it. I couldn't wait to see what dishes would arrive on the day of our party!

"My family loves Italian food," said Sophia on the morning of the party. "I brought spaghetti and meatballs."

"This is our favorite," said Sam. "It's lamb curry from India."

"Wait until you taste my Mexican tamales," said Elena.

I looked at all the strange dishes with great **curiosity**. Mr. Ortiz watched me **gaze** at each dish. He thought I was **untrusting**. "I can't wait to try some of these foods, Mr. Ortiz," I said.

I tried chicken stew from Kenya, German sausages, Greek salad, and more. All of it was delicious!

Not only did I eat a world of food, I met a world of families, too. We all did. What a day!

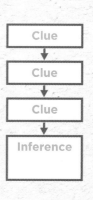

Reread for **Comprehension**

Visualize

STRATEGY SKILL

Make Inferences

Authors don't always tell you exactly what the character in a story is thinking. You need to use story clues and what you already know to figure it out. This is called making inferences. Visualizing, or picturing, what the author tells you can help you make inferences.

Reread the selection to make inferences about the narrator's opinion of the class party. Use the Inference Map to help you.

Clue
Clue
Clue
Inference

Comprehension

Genre

A **Folktale** is a story based on the customs and traditions of a people or region, handed down orally from one generation to the next.

Visualize

Make Inferences

As you read, use your Inference Map.

```
┌─────────────┐
│    Clue     │
└─────────────┘
       ↓
┌─────────────┐
│    Clue     │
└─────────────┘
       ↓
┌─────────────┐
│    Clue     │
└─────────────┘
       ↓
┌─────────────┐
│  Inference  │
│             │
└─────────────┘
```

Read to Find Out

What lesson does making stone soup teach the people in the village?

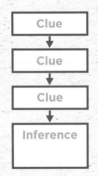

STONE SOUP

Award Winning Author

retold and
illustrated by
Jon J Muth

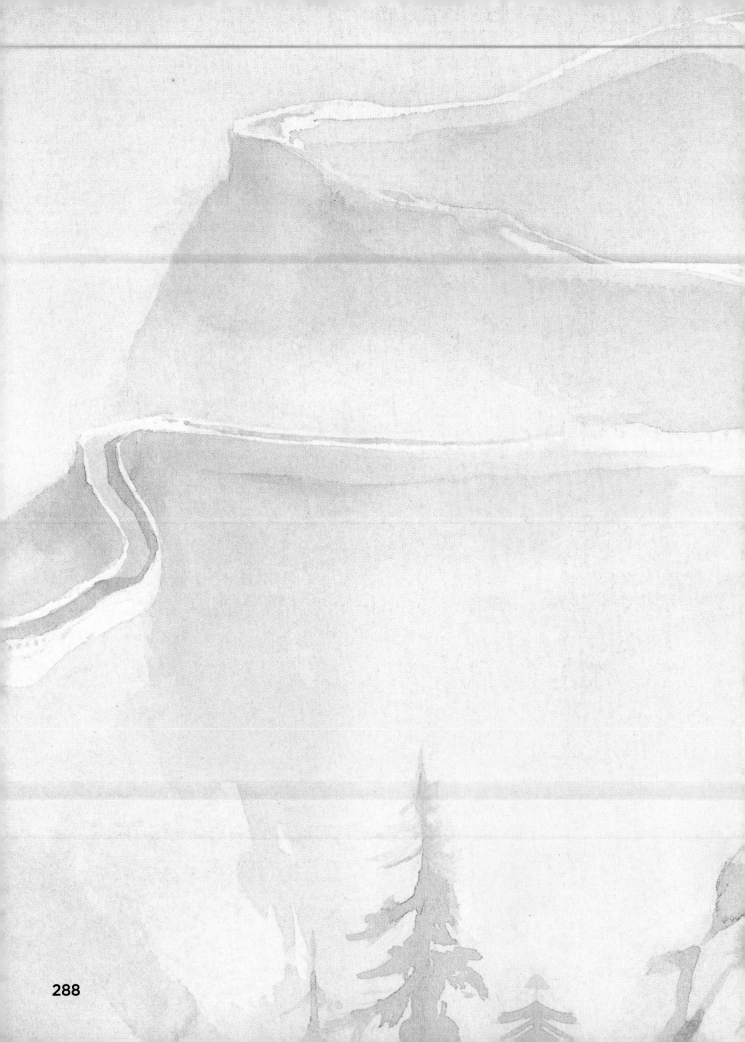

288

THREE MONKS, Hok, Lok, and Siew, traveled along a mountain road. They talked about cat whiskers, the color of the sun, and giving.

"What makes one happy, Siew?" asked Hok, the youngest monk.

Old Siew, who was the wisest, said, "Let's find out."

Make Inferences
What do you think makes the monks happy?

The sound of a bell brought their **gaze** to the rooftops of a village below. They could not see from so high above that the village had been through many hard times. Famine, floods, and war had made the villagers weary and **untrusting** of strangers. They had even become suspicious of their neighbors.

The villagers worked hard, but only for themselves.

There was a farmer.

A tea merchant.

A scholar.

A seamstress.

A doctor.

A carpenter ...
... and many others.
But they had little to do with
one another.

When the monks reached the foot of the mountain, the villagers disappeared into their houses. No one came to the gates to greet them.

And when the people saw them enter the village, they closed their windows tight.

The monks knocked on the door of the first house. There was no answer. Then the house went dark.

They knocked on a second door and the same thing happened.

It happened again and again, from one house to the next.

"These people do not know happiness," they all agreed.

"But today," said Siew, his face bright as the moon, "we will show them how to make stone soup."

Make Inferences
Why do the monks say that the villagers are not happy?

They gathered twigs and branches and made a fire.

They placed a small tin pot on top and filled it with water from the village well.

A brave little girl who had been watching came to them. "What are you doing?" she asked.

"We are gathering twigs," said Lok.

"We are making a fire," said Hok.

"We are making stone soup and we need three round, smooth stones," said Siew.

The little girl helped the monks look around the courtyard until they found just the right ones. Then they put them in the water to cook.

"These stones will make excellent soup," said Siew. "But this very small pot won't make much I'm afraid."

"My mother has a bigger pot," said the girl.

The little girl ran home. As she started to take a pot, her mother asked what she was doing.

"The three strangers are making soup from stones," she said. "They need our biggest pot."

"Hmm," said the girl's mother. "Stones are easy to come by. I'd like to learn how to do that!"

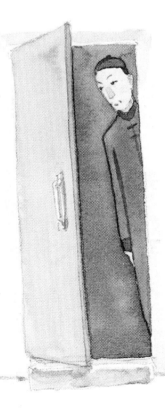

The monks poked the coals. As smoke drifted up, the neighbors peered out from their windows. The fire and the large pot in the middle of the village was a true **curiosity**!

One by one, the people of the village came out to see just what this stone soup was.

297

"Of course, old-style stone soup should be well seasoned with salt and pepper," said Hok.

"That is true," said Lok as he stirred the giant pot filled with water and stones. "But we have none ..."

"I have some salt and pepper!" said the scholar, his eyes big with curiosity. He disappeared and came back with salt and pepper and even a few other spices.

Siew took a taste. "The last time we had soup stones of this size and color, carrots made the broth very sweet."

"Carrots?" said a woman from the back. "I may have a few carrots! But just a few." And off she ran. She returned with as many carrots as she could carry and dropped them into the pot.

"Do you think it would be better with onions?" asked Hok.

"Oh, yes, maybe an onion would taste good," said a farmer, and he hurried off. He returned in a moment with five big onions, and he dropped them into the bubbling soup.

"Now, that's a fine soup!" he said.

The villagers all nodded their heads, as the smell was very **agreeable**.

"But if only we had some mushrooms," said Siew, rubbing his chin.

Several villagers licked their lips. A few dashed away and returned with fresh mushrooms, noodles, pea pods, and cabbages.

Something magical began to happen among the villagers. As each person opened their heart to give, the next person gave even more. And as this happened, the soup grew richer and smelled more delicious.

"I imagine the Emperor would suggest we add dumplings!" said one villager.

"And bean curd!" said another.

"What about cloud ear and mung beans and yams?" cried some others.

"And taro root and winter melon and baby corn!" cried other villagers.

"Garlic!" "Ginger Root!" "Soy sauce!" "Lily buds!"

"I have some! I have some!" people cried out. And off they ran, returning with all they could carry.

The monks stirred and the pot bubbled. How
good it smelled! How good it would taste! How
giving the villagers had become!

At last, the soup was ready. The villagers gathered together. They brought rice and steamed buns. They brought lychee nuts and sweet cakes. They brought tea to drink, and they lit lanterns.

Everyone sat down to eat. They had not been together for a feast like this for as long as anyone could remember.

After the **banquet**, they told stories, sang songs, and celebrated long into the night.

Then they unlocked their doors and took the monks into their homes and gave them very comfortable places to sleep.

In the gentle spring morning, everyone gathered together near the willows to say farewell.

"Thank you for having us as your **guests**," said the monks. "You have been most generous."

"Thank you," said the villagers. "With the gifts you have given, we will always have plenty. You have shown us that sharing makes us all richer."

"And to think," said the monks, "to be happy is as simple as making stone soup."

Make Inferences
What will it take for this happiness to continue?

The Soup on Jon J Muth

Jon J Muth can take old stories and turn them into new ones by setting them in different places. He took an old tale from Europe to write this Chinese story. When Jon was a boy, his mother took him to museums all across the United States. Later, he studied art in Asia and Europe. As Jon illustrates a book, he imagines that he is a boy running around inside the story. Then he can see things the way a child does.

Other books by Jon J Muth: *Come On, Rain!* and *The Three Questions*

LOG ON Find out more about Jon J Muth at **www.macmillanmh.com**

Write About It

This story begins with the three monks thinking about what makes a person happy. Write about what makes you happy.

Comprehension Check

TEST PREP

Summarize

Summarize what the monks did in *Stone Soup*. Use your Inference Map to help you explain why they wanted to make the soup.

Clue
↓
Clue
↓
Clue
↓
Inference

Think and Compare

1. What details in the story show why the monks thought that making stone soup would bring happiness to the **untrusting** villagers? Use your Inference Map to gather clues. **Visualize: Make Inferences**

2. Examine the pictures of the villagers on pages 290–291. What do you notice about their expressions? Why did Jon J Muth draw them this way? **Analyze**

3. What is your opinion about sharing something as part of a group? Explain your answer. **Evaluate**

4. What facts would you choose to show how the world might change if more people shared? Explain your answer. **Apply**

5. Read "Family Feast" on pages 284–285. Compare the class banquet to the village feast in *Stone Soup*. How are they alike? How are they different? Use details from both selections in your answer. **Reading/Writing Across Texts**

What's for Lunch?

by Leonard Mercury

What will you eat for lunch today? In some countries, lunchtime often means soup time! There are many kinds of **unique**, or different, soups served around the world. Some are as thin and clear as water. Some are as thick as stews. Others are full of noodles!

Soup is just one thing that can be eaten for lunch. What you eat for lunch may be different from the lunch of someone who lives in another country. Let's take a look around the world to see what kids are eating for lunch.

Mexico: Tasting Tortillas

Many children in Mexico eat **tortillas** (tor·TEE·yas) for lunch. Most tortillas are made from ground corn, but sometimes wheat flour is used. Tortillas are usually flat and round, but they can also be made into other shapes. Taco shells are made from corn tortillas and filled with beans or meat. Tasty sauces, called salsas, are often added to tacos. These sauces are made from chopped tomatoes, onions, hot peppers, and spices. Salsas add flavor and vitamins.

Russia: Sipping Soup

Winters in Russia are very cold. Maybe that's why many Russian children eat soup for lunch. Two of their favorites are cabbage soup and beet soup.

Many Russian soups also include potatoes. Potatoes are an important crop in Russia. They make soups thick and **hearty**. Eating thick soups can help keep people warm and can fill them up so hunger is no problem!

School Lunches Around the World

SKILL

Reading a Chart

Charts organize ideas into columns and rows.

This chart has two headings in the first row: "Country" and "School Lunches." Down the first column, you can read the country names. The second column shows what is eaten in each place.

column

Country	School Lunches
Russia	beet or potato soup; wheat or rye bread	row
Mexico	tortillas with black beans and salsa
India	chapatis with dal
Thailand	rice noodles with tofu, shrimp, and peanuts
South Korea	squid with hot sauce, rice, radish kimchi

South Korea: Passing the Pickles

Meals in Korea are made up of many dishes. No matter what else is served, there is always rice.

Kimchi (KIM·chee) is also always on the table. Kimchi is pickled meat or vegetables. Korean children mix together many dishes and flavors at meals. It's common for their food to be hot and spicy.

Thailand:
Eating Noodles at Noon

Lunch in Thailand often includes noodles. There are many ways to serve noodles. One popular dish is made with thin rice noodles, tofu, and shrimp. Another favorite way to eat rice noodles is with meat, vegetables, and thick gravy.

India: Chewing on Chapatis

Many children living in India eat **chapatis** (chuh·PAH·tees) for lunch. Chapatis are made from only two ingredients: wheat flour and water. The flour and water are mixed into dough. The dough is rolled flat and thin. It's cooked on a hot griddle until it puffs up. Then it's held over an open flame.

Some children like dal (dahl) with their chapatis. Dal looks like a very thick soup. It is spicy and delicious!

Connect and Compare

1. Look at the chart on page 309. What kind of soups do children eat for school lunch in Russia? **Reading a Chart**

2. Based on what you know, where in the world would you like to eat lunch? Explain your answer. **Evaluate**

3. Think about this article and *Stone Soup*. What ingredients might people from Russia, Mexico, India, Thailand, and South Korea have brought to put in the soup? **Reading/Writing Across Texts**

Social Studies Activity

Learn what kids eat for lunch in a country not on the chart, such as Australia, Iran, or Greece. Copy the chart and add your new row of information to it.

 Find out more about lunch at **www.macmillanmh.com**

Write a Journal Entry

Writing

Voice

Your writing voice shows how you feel about your topic. It can show interest and excitement.

I wrote a journal entry about a meal in a Chinese restaurant.

I used the same kind of action verbs that I use when I speak.

Dim Sum Sunday

by Jerry S.

October 12, 20--

Today we went to a Chinese restaurant to have dim sum, or dumplings. I have never had dim sum before. A waiter brought out a plate with five little dumplings on it. I looked nervously at the pale dough, but I was starving. I grabbed a fork and tasted one. It was so good! I quickly reached for another, but Dad said we had to share. Just then, the waiter slid five more plates of dim sum onto the table. Whew!

Your Turn

Write a journal entry about an experience you have had with food. It may be about the best meal you have ever eaten. It may be about a special meal that you helped prepare. Be sure to express your individual voice in your paragraph. Use the Writer's Checklist to check your writing.

Writer's Checklist

☑ **Ideas and Content:** Did I write about something that happened to me?

☑ **Organization:** Did I tell the events in order?

  ☐ Voice: When I read my writing aloud, does it sound the way I talk?

☑ **Word Choice:** Did I use action words?

☑ **Sentence Fluency:** Did I vary the lengths of my sentences?

☑ **Conventions:** Did I use commas correctly in dates and place names? Did I check my spelling?

SOLVING RIDDLES

Talk About It

Riddles are word puzzles. What was the last riddle you tried to solve?

LOG ON Find out more about solving riddles at **www.macmillanmh.com**

315

Vocabulary

wearily	observed
depart	advised
suitable	discouraged
increase	

Dictionary

Unfamiliar Words can be looked up in a dictionary to find their meanings.

Use a dictionary to find out what the word *suitable* means.

Count On Detective Drake!

by Arthur Stamos

Detective Drake was napping with his feet up on his desk when the phone rang. He yawned and picked it up. "Hello?" he said **wearily**. "I'll take the case. I will **depart** at once." Drake grabbed his umbrella, which was **suitable** for the rain outside, and walked out into the noisy city.

The Case

Drake pulled up to the police station. "We've been getting unfinished math problems in the mail," the Chief said. "They're signed 'Guessss Who?' Every day the number of letters **increase**. We keep getting more. They are clogging up the mail room."

Drake looked at the paper in the Chief's hand. He **observed** one letter's clue:

$\square$ + 32 = 51 Guessss Who?

Gathering Clues

"The word *guess* isn't spelled right," Drake said thoughtfully. "Give me the clues, Chief," he said. "And if someone asks you, say that I've **advised** you not to discuss the case. If you do what I say, I'll get this problem solved quickly."

Drake took the clues and went back to his office. First, he filled in the missing numbers. Then, he wrote the numbers in a notebook:

1 1 5 5 5 8 10 11 11 14 19 20

"Is it a code?" he thought aloud. "Think, Drake, think!" "Maybe it's an alphabet code!" Drake shouted. When he matched the numbers to the letters of the alphabet, this is what he had:

A A E E E H J K K N S T

Case Solved!

"This doesn't add up," he said, disappointed and **discouraged**. He kept moving the letters around. Finally, he had it: JAKE THE SNAKE.

Drake called the Chief. "That snake, Jake, is your man."

"I knew I could *count* on you!" said the Chief.

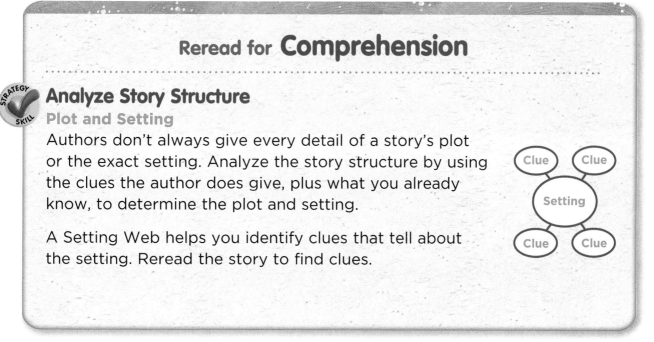

Reread for Comprehension

Analyze Story Structure
Plot and Setting
Authors don't always give every detail of a story's plot or the exact setting. Analyze the story structure by using the clues the author does give, plus what you already know, to determine the plot and setting.

A Setting Web helps you identify clues that tell about the setting. Reread the story to find clues.

Comprehension

Genre

Fairy Tales take place long ago and have imaginary characters and settings.

Analyze Story Structure

Plot and Setting

As you read, use your Setting Web.

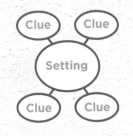

Read to Find Out

Where in the world does Aziza live?

318

One Riddle, One Answer

by Lauren Thompson

illustrated by Linda S. Wingerter

$\mathcal{L}$ong ago in Persia, there lived a powerful sultan. He had many sons, but only one daughter, named Aziza, and he wished for her a wise and happy life. The finest tutors in the land were brought to the palace, and Aziza learned all there was to know. But her favorite subject was numbers. And her favorite game was riddles.

Plot and Setting

When and where does this story take place?

The time came for Aziza to marry. The sultan began to seek a **suitable** husband for her.

"Who in the land is most worthy of her hand?" the sultan asked his advisors.

"My eldest son is very handsome, your honor," said one advisor.

"My youngest son is very clever," said another.

It seemed that all of the sultan's advisors had only their own sons to recommend. The sultan was angry.

"You have **advised** enough!" cried the sultan, and he sent his advisors away.

Then Aziza went to the sultan.

"Father," she said, "perhaps there is a better way to choose whom I should marry."

The sultan knew his daughter was wise and good, and above all he wished her to be happy. "Tell me your plan," he said.

"Let me pose a riddle," said Aziza. "The riddle has but one true answer. Whoever can answer the riddle will be the one I would be happiest to marry."

"A riddle?" asked the sultan.

"Yes," said Aziza. "Here it is."

Placed above, it makes great things small.
Placed beside, it makes small things greater.
In matters that count, it always comes first.
Where others increase, it keeps all things the same.
What is it?

The sultan thought for a moment, and then he sighed. "This riddle is too difficult even for me. In all the land, there is no man who will solve this riddle."

"Perhaps there will be one," Aziza said. "And one is all that is needed."

So the sultan agreed to Aziza's plan.

The next day, Aziza set out with a caravan in search of the one who could solve the riddle. In every city, town, and village, a messenger spread the news of the sultan's daughter's riddle.

"One riddle, one answer! Let any number try!" cried the messenger. "Only one will win the hand of the sultan's daughter!"

Every place they stopped, men young and old tried to solve the riddle. But none had the answer.

STRATEGY SKILL

Plot and Setting
Where does Aziza go on the caravan and why?

325

In one village, a scholar came before Aziza to announce his answer. He was an astronomer, who studied the movements of the sun, moon, and stars.

"I have **observed** that the answer is the sun," he said with much confidence. "For the riddle speaks of shadows. When the sun is high above us, even the greatest man seems small, as he has only a small shadow. Thus, the answer is the sun."

"A learned answer indeed," said Aziza. "But that is not the right answer to the riddle."

In another town, a soldier came before Aziza with his answer.

"A sword!" he cried, displaying his gleaming saber. "The answer must be a sword. For the riddle speaks of war. And in war, even the smallest man is great in strength with a sword by his side."

"You have given a strong answer," said Aziza. "But that is not the right answer to the riddle."

In another city, a merchant came before Aziza.

"Honored lady," he said sweetly, "your clever riddle has been solved. The riddle speaks of the ways of the world, and the answer, therefore, is money. For as everyone knows, in all matters that count, money always comes first." He smiled at Aziza, sure that he had won her hand.

"Your answer is more clever than my riddle," said Aziza **wearily**. "But your clever answer is wrong."

"May I try another riddle?" asked the merchant.

"No," Aziza said. "One riddle, one answer."

Aziza felt **discouraged**. Perhaps her father was right. Perhaps no one in the land would know the answer to the riddle. She ordered the caravan to return to her father's palace.

Just as the caravan was about to **depart**, a young man came forward. He was a farmer named Ahmed, and he too loved numbers.

"Will you hear one more answer?" Ahmed asked.

"Just one more," Aziza said, sighing.

"The riddle speaks of numbers," he said, "and the answer is the number one. For in a fraction, the number one placed above a large number makes a small number. One hundred is large, but one hundredth is small."

"Yes, it is," said Aziza. "Go on."

"And when the number one is placed beside another number," he said, "the number increases. One placed beside nine makes nineteen."

"Or ninety-one," said Aziza. She smiled.

"Or ninety-one," said Ahmed. He smiled back.

"And in counting," Ahmed went on, "the number one always comes first. That is as simple as one, two, three."

"Yes!" said Aziza, laughing.

Ahmed said, "And in multiplication, the number one keeps the value of another number, while other numbers increase the value. One times ten is ten, but two times ten is twenty, and three times ten is thirty. And this is why," said Ahmed, "the answer to your riddle is the number one."

"That is a wonderful answer," said Aziza. "And it is right! With this answer, you have won my hand."

"With this riddle, you have won my heart," said Ahmed.

Aziza and Ahmed returned to the sultan's palace. Before long, they were married.

The sultan made Ahmed his chief advisor in matters of farming.

And he made Aziza his chief advisor in matters of numbers.

By the Numbers with Lauren and Linda

Author **Lauren Thompson** is a lot like Aziza. She has loved words and numbers ever since she was a girl. Lauren put her two favorite things together to write this riddle story. She set her story in Persia (the country now called Iran) because that is where many important math ideas began.

Other books by Lauren Thompson: *Little Quack's Hide and Seek* and *Mouse's First Summer*

Illustrator **Linda S. Wingerter** has illustrated many books for children. Besides being an artist, Linda has another talent: she is an excellent skater, and she enjoys doing it very much.

LOG ON Find out more about Lauren Thompson and Linda S. Wingerter at **www.macmillanmh.com**

Write About It

Aziza and author Lauren Thompson love to play with numbers. Describe how you have fun with numbers, or how they help you every day.

Comprehension Check

Summarize

Summarize Aziza's search for a husband in *One Riddle, One Answer*. Be sure to describe the setting and plot. Use your Setting Web to help you.

Clue — Clue — Setting — Clue — Clue

Think and Compare

1. How does the setting influence the story and Aziza's search for a husband? **Analyze Story Structure: Plot and Setting**

2. Why would the man who can answer her riddle be a **suitable** husband for Aziza? Use story details in your answer. **Analyze**

3. If you were to meet Ahmed, what questions would you ask him? **Apply**

4. Based on what you know, why do people like to have friends with the same interests as theirs? Explain your answer. **Evaluate**

5. Read "Count on Detective Drake!" on pages 316–317. How is it similar to *One Riddle, One Answer*? In what ways is the main character's behavior different? Use details from both selections in your answer. **Reading/Writing Across Texts**

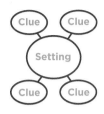

Haiku

Poetry

Haiku is a poem about nature that describes a moment or scene in three lines. The first and third lines have five syllables each; the second line has seven.

✓SKILL

Literary Elements

Consonance is the repetition of the same consonant sound at the end of two or more words.

A **metaphor** compares two different things so they seem to be alike.

Broken and broken
Again on the sea, the moon
So easily mends.

—Chosu

Calling an umbrella a "tent" is an example of a metaphor.

Shiny colored tents
Pop up above people's heads
At the first raindrop.

—Myra Cohn Livingston

A lonely sparrow
Hops upon the snow and prints
Sets of maple leaves.

—*Kazue Mizumura*

Hops, prints, and *sets* all end with the same sound to create consonance.

Connect and Compare

1. In the haiku by Kazue Mizumura, what two things are being compared by metaphor? **Metaphor**

2. How do you know what moment or scene is described in the haiku by Myra Cohn Livingston? **Evaluate**

3. *One Riddle, One Answer* is about a riddle. How are these haiku like riddles? **Reading/Writing Across Texts**

LOG ON Find out more about haiku at **www.macmillanmh.com**

337

Write a Character Sketch

Elva the Elf

by Vanessa G.

Elva the pink-haired elf is so smart that she can solve any problem. Elftown would fall apart without her! She fixes all of the town's cars and computers. She even flies the town plane. Best of all, Elva got rid of creepy Walter Wolf. He wanted to eat the elves for dinner. When Walter Wolf came around, Elva blasted the volume on her radio. It was so loud the wolf covered his ears and ran away for good. All the elves cheered for Elva.

I made up a fairy tale character called Elva. I described how clever Elva is.

I used precise, active verbs.

Your Turn

Write a character sketch about a smart fairy tale character. In a paragraph, explain what makes the character so smart. Be sure to use precise, active verbs to describe what the character does. Use the Writer's Checklist to check your writing.

Writer's Checklist

☑ **Ideas and Content:** Did I give enough details?

☑ **Organization:** Does the title I chose fit?

☑ **Voice:** Will the reader know how I feel about the character?

☐ **Word Choice:** Did I use precise, active verbs to tell what my character does?

☑ **Sentence Fluency:** Did I avoid using sentence fragments?

☑ **Conventions:** Did I use present-tense verbs correctly and check for subject-verb agreement? Did I check my spelling?

Talk About It

Ecosystems are communities of plants and animals. How do people's activities affect these communities?

LOG ON Find out more about ecosystems at **www.macmillanmh.com**

ECOSYSTEMS IN BALANCE

Vocabulary

preserve
restore
suffered
rainfall

Putting up bluebird houses at the Kern River Preserve

For the Birds!

The Kern River **Preserve** keeps the environment safe for the plants and animals that live there, but some parts of the preserve are being destroyed or lost. The kids in Cassie Wingender's class at Woodrow Wallace Elementary School came up with a plan to help **restore**, or return part of the preserve to its natural state.

The mountain bluebird likes to move into empty woodpecker nests in trees. As trees get old, they fall or have to be cut down. The birds have **suffered** because their nests are destroyed or lost. The students built 21 birdhouses that are designed to attract bluebirds and keep out other animals.

Southwestern willow flycatchers had nowhere to lay their eggs and protect them, so the students planted 50 cottonwood trees.

The students plan to do more. They want to **preserve** the forest, or keep it safe, so that it will be there in the future, for their own children to enjoy.

Find out more about ecosystems at **www.macmillanmh.com**

342

The Desert Is Alive!

The Chihuahuan (chee•WAH•wahn) Desert stretches across the southwestern United States and part of Mexico. The ground is hot and cracked. Nearly every plant has thorns or needles. Still, almost 1,000 species of animals live there.

The desert's increasing human population has become a problem. Some farmers and ranchers allow their cattle to graze at the wrong time of year, which harms desert grasses.

Jim Winder divided part of his land into small pastures. He moves cattle to a different grazing spot every few days. This keeps the grass healthy. Winder also restored a lake. Now more than 100 species of water-loving birds live there.

One rancher can't save a huge desert. Still, Jim Winder likes how his grass is growing. "It looks good for grazing," he says with a smile.

Jim Winder

The Chihuahuan Desert

TFK TOP 5 DESERTS

Deserts are the driest places on the planet. A desert may only get about 10 inches of **rainfall** a year. Some deserts are hot, such as the Sahara Desert in Africa.

Some deserts are cold but still very dry, such as the Gobi Desert in Asia. Here is a list of the largest deserts in the world.

1. Sahara (Africa)	3,500,000 square miles	(9,065,000 sq km)
2. Arabian (Asia)	1,000,000 square miles	(2,600,000 sq km)
3. Australian	570,000 square miles	(1,476,000 sq km)
4. Gobi (Asia)	500,000 square miles	(1,295,000 sq km)
5. Kalahari (Africa)	225,000 square miles	(582,700 sq km)

Saving the Sand Dunes

Comprehension

Genre

Nonfiction Articles give information about real people, places, or things.

Analyze Text Structure

Cause and Effect

A cause is why something happens. An effect is what happens.

How can items be recycled to help the environment?

Christmas trees can protect the sand dunes.

The mighty wind whirled. Waves crashed and pounded the beach. Sand was swept up into the air and blew away. Still nothing could topple the science project of Tony Pontari's fourth-grade class at Union Avenue School in New Jersey. Their hand-built sand dune held tough through winter storms, helping to protect Grandville Avenue Beach and the town of Margate, New Jersey.

In many beachfront towns, dunes work as a windbreaker. They help stop the wind from blowing beach sand away. They stop the ocean water from spilling past the beach.

However, big storms cause many dunes to disappear. For years, the dunes at Margate **suffered** from the effects of winter storms. People tried to strengthen them by laying trees sideways on the sand. Those trees were usually swept out to sea.

Students check on the trees they buried at Grandville Avenue Beach.

A Recycled Forest Fights Erosion

One year, the fourth-grade class of Union Avenue School decided to try something new. The students found a way to reuse dead trees that are usually thrown away after the Christmas season. They buried the trees standing up in three trenches, each 100 feet long.

The recycled trees kept the new dune in place through the winter. Big winter storms washed away other sand dunes, but the dunes at Margate held together because of the buried trees.

Since it worked so well, the following year's fourth-grade class decided to continue the project. By then they had partners. Teacher Kevin Burns from nearby Brigantine Middle School had heard about the kid-made dune in Margate. He wanted his students to build one, too.

Because of the success of their plan, the kids got help from town officials. After Christmas, workers for the towns of Margate and Brigantine collected used trees. The workers took the trees down to the two towns' beaches. They dug three-foot-deep trenches, then the students planted the trees.

"The trees were heavy, and some were bigger than me," says fourth-grader Jim Abbott. But the kids had fun, too. "Sometimes we found Christmas lights!" says Kara Weiner, another fourth-grader.

Because the kids buried only the lower half of each tree in the sand, the upper half acted as a sand catcher. It trapped windblown sand until the tree was completely buried. The students then tied red ribbons to the treetops.

Town workers deliver discarded Christmas trees to the beach.

A Home for Native Species

Sand dunes help protect the shoreline ecosystem. In some places, dunes are part of a nature **preserve**, but all dunes need to be protected.

Dunes provide habitats for marine species. That's one reason to **restore** dunes that have been washed away.

Dunes also help protect the homes of nearby residents from flooding when storms bring heavy **rainfall**, high tides, and huge waves. Dunes also keep the sand where it belongs: on the beach!

Sand dunes are an important part of the beach ecosystem.

Next, they checked the buildup of sand by measuring the distance between the end of each ribbon and the top of the growing dune. The two schools communicated by e-mail to compare results.

In the spring, when the dunes had collected enough sand, the classes planted dune grass on top of them. The roots of the grass grow down and anchor the dunes. Town workers then placed wooden fences around the sand to help pack the sand together so the dunes are protected.

Think and Compare

STRATEGY SKILL ✓

1. Why did students "plant" dead trees on the beach?

2. What effect did planting trees have on the beachfront towns?

3. Have you ever found a new use for an old object? Describe it.

4. What do the Kern River Preserve, Chihuahuan Desert, and sand dunes in New Jersey all have in common?

347

Frog Frenzy!

Nate Egan and an amphibian friend

Barking Tree Frog

American Bullfrog

Northern Leopard Frog

Ribbit, ribbit. When that sound echoes across the pond behind Nate Egan's house in Oregon, Illinois, he knows what's making it. Frogs. A lot of them. However, across the United States, there are fewer green jumpers than there once were. Worried scientists have seen the number of frogs dropping since the late 1980s. That's why Nate, 9, and more than 3,800 other kids and adults are volunteering for Frogwatch USA. They listen to frog calls during the spring and summer. Then they report their observations online to scientists.

Amy Goodstine is the coordinator of Frogwatch USA. She says that pollution, pesticides, global warming, and the loss of habitats are among the factors threatening the frog population.

The U.S. Geological Survey (USGS) started Frogwatch USA in 1999. Its purpose was to try to find out why frogs are growing scarcer. In 2001, the USGS and the National Wildlife Federation started working together on this project.

Go On

Directions: Answer the questions.

1. **Why are Frogwatch volunteers listening to frogs?**

   A to help find out why the number of frogs is decreasing

   B to become experts at identifying kinds of frogs

   C so they can repeat the sounds

   D to earn money and be close to nature

2. **What effect have pollution and pesticides had on the frog population?**

   A Frogs will soon become extinct.

   B The frogs have lost their habitats.

   C There are too many frogs in the spring.

   D There are fewer frogs now than before.

3. **What is the purpose of Frogwatch USA?**

   A to report frog calls during the spring and summer

   B to learn more about using computers

   C to get frogs to return to ponds

   D to figure out how to protect the frog population

4. **How do scientists get information from Frogwatch volunteers?**

5. **What are the possible reasons why the number of frogs is dropping? What could be done to protect the frogs in the future? Use details from the article to support your answer.**

> **Tip**
> Look for information in more than one place.

Write to a Prompt

In the selection "For the Birds!" you read about what one class is doing to try to restore a habitat and protect birds. Imagine you are in that class. Write a letter to your teacher to explain why more classes should get involved in the project.

I started my writing with a good topic sentence to persuade my reader.

I wrote sentences that support my argument.

November 7, 20--

Dear Mrs. Wynn,

   We need to take care of Kern River Preserve because it is a home for birds, animals, and people, too. If we don't, the birds will die. The forest will not be as special. People will be sad.

   Old trees are falling down, and people cut down the good ones. There aren't enough trees for bluebirds to build their nests. We can build birdhouses for them. Southwestern willow flycatchers need help, too. If we plant more cottonwood trees for them, their eggs will be safe.

   Kern River Preserve is a special place. All our classes should help to keep it that way.

                    Sincerely,
                    Zachary K.

350

Writing Prompt

In the selection "Saving the Sand Dunes" you read about what's being done to protect beaches in towns near the shore. Imagine that you lived in a town near the seashore. Write a letter to a friend describing why "planting" used Christmas trees would be a good project for kids in your school and for the town. Use examples to support your argument.

Writer's Checklist

- ☑ Ask yourself, who is my audience?
- ☑ Think about your purpose for writing.
- ☑ Form an opinion about the topic.
- ☑ Use reasons to support your opinion.
- ☑ Be sure your ideas are logical and organized.
- ☑ Use your best spelling, grammar, and punctuation.

Making Journeys

Vocabulary

annual	package
potential	wrapping
expensive	innocent
politely	aisles

Dictionary

Homophones are words that sound the same but have different meanings and spellings. The words *wrapping* and *rapping* are homophones.

My Winter Vacation

by Meredith Gamel

December 22

We're leaving for Florida to visit Aunt Sue, Uncle Mike, and my cousins Tim and Laura. We go every year over the holidays. I guess you could call this our **annual** trip. The trip has the **potential** for being fun, but I'd rather celebrate at home. Dad's rushing me, so I'd better hurry.

December 23

We're almost there. Last night we stayed at a hotel. Dad said it was **expensive**, but Mom said she didn't care what it cost, she needed a break from being in the car. I got to swim in the hotel pool. It felt good after sitting in the car all day.

December 26

We have been at Aunt Sue's for two days. Yesterday she made lobsters for lunch. They looked terrible—like big, red bugs! I **politely** said, "No, thank you. I'm sticking with tuna!"

Today I found a **package** covered in brown paper on my bed. It was from Grandma. I took off the **wrapping** paper. It's a wave board! Time to go to the beach and try it out. Yay!

December 28

I love the ocean, but the water is freezing! Laura dumped a pail of water on my dad. Boy, did he jump! She tried to look sweet and **innocent**, but Dad knew she had done it. She does it every year!

December 30

Last day at the beach. I wish we didn't have to go. Anyway, school starts in a few days, and Mom says we need to go grocery shopping. While I'm going up and down the food **aisles**, I'll think about the beach and look forward to using my wave board again.

Reread for **Comprehension**

STRATEGY ✓ SKILL

Visualize

Make Inferences

Authors don't always tell you exactly how a character in a story is feeling. You need to use story clues and what you already know. This is called making inferences. Visualizing what the author tells you can help you make inferences.

Reread the selection to make inferences about whether the journal writer had fun at the beach. Use the Inference Chart to help you.

Clues	Inference

THE JONES

Award
Winning
Illustrator

Comprehension

Genre

Realistic Fiction is an invented story that could have happened in real life.

Visualize

Make Inferences
As you read, use your Inference Chart.

Clues	Inference

Read to Find Out

How will Steven get a gift for his aunt?

FAMILY EXPRESS

WRITTEN AND ILLUSTRATED BY JAVAKA STEPTOE

Every summer for as long as I can remember, my Aunt Carolyn has gone traveling. Sometimes she would go out of the country and other times she just got on a train and visited different places. She always had funny stories to tell when she returned.

I thought Aunt Carolyn's stories were so much fun that once, when I was three, I hid in her suitcase so she would take me with her. She was so tickled, she promised to send me a postcard from every place she went until I was old enough to travel with her. Grandma had to read the postcards to me at first, but as I got older, I read them myself.

Those postcards always made me feel special.

STRATEGY SKILL

Make Inferences
How does Aunt Carolyn feel about the narrator? How can you tell?

This summer Aunt Carolyn said she would be here for our **annual** block party. The block party was my favorite time of the year because the whole family visited us at Grandma's house. People came from everywhere, and there was a lot of food, music, and things to do.

Aunt Carolyn didn't come back often, so I wanted to get something special for her. I just didn't know what.

The night before the party, I barely got any sleep. My cousin Sean was staying over, and I had to share my bed with him. Sean was always asking questions.

"Why do dogs like dog biscuits?" he asked.

"I don't know," I answered, but I wasn't really listening. I just lay there thinking until I came up with an idea. Maybe I could find something for Aunt Carolyn on Nostrand Avenue! You can buy almost anything there.

The next morning I woke up to the smell of Grandma's pancakes.

"Get up, Sean," I said, poking him in his ribs. "It's time to get up!" We got dressed and ran downstairs.

"Good morning, Grandma," we sang as we sat down to heaping plates of her buttery-syrupy pancakes.

Uncle Charles walked in, grumpy as usual. Sean and I covered our plates with our arms because Uncle Charles liked to take bites of your food.

"Stop it, Charles," Grandma said just as he reached for one of my pancakes.

"I only do it out of love," Uncle Charles replied, acting all **innocent**. "I want to make sure it's not poisoned."

In between bites Sean told Grandma how he'd been working on a rap for the block party talent show.

Suddenly the phone rang.

"Hey, Carolyn," Grandma said in her cheery voice. "When are you getting in?... The 2:30 train? You need anything?... All right then, we'll see you soon."

I looked at my watch. I had only about four and a half hours until Aunt Carolyn arrived!

Just then Aunt Marsha walked in carrying three big bags of potatoes.

I looked at Sean. "We better get out of here before they have us peeling potatoes," I whispered.

When we reached the vestibule door, we heard country music blasting. That could mean only one thing. Granddad! I didn't want to get trapped having to help Granddad make his secret barbecue sauce that everybody knew the secret to. Besides, Granddad liked to tell long stories.

"Sean," I said. "Go talk to Granddad. I'll be out in a minute."

As soon as Sean was gone, I ran up to my room, climbed out the window onto our neighbor's toolshed, and made my way past her garden to the street. Then I headed toward Nostrand Avenue.

Chicago
The center of Chicago's Grant Park, Buck
Fountain is of the most regularly visited attractions of
Chicago.
in any form without p
hat igni

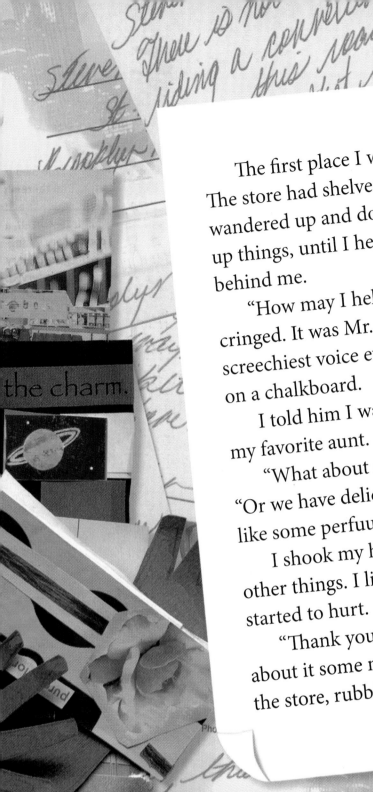

The first place I went was Perkins Drugstore. The store had shelves and shelves of stuff. I wandered up and down the **aisles**, picking up things, until I heard someone come up behind me.

"How may I help you, young maaaaan?" I cringed. It was Mr. Perkins, the owner. He had the screechiest voice ever. It was like nails scratching on a chalkboard.

I told him I wanted to find a special gift for my favorite aunt.

"What about some caaards?" Mr. Perkins said. "Or we have delicious chocolaaaates. She might like some perfuuuume."

I shook my head no, so he started suggesting other things. I listened **politely** until my head started to hurt.

"Thank you," I said finally. "Let me think about it some more." Then I walked quickly out of the store, rubbing my ears.

Next I went to Ms. Ruby's shop. She's from Jamaica. She had lots of handmade things in her store, and I loved the way she talked.

"Hey, sweetie. How you do?" Ms. Ruby asked.

"I'm looking for a surprise for my Aunt Carolyn," I answered, looking around the shop. "I've saved up ten dollars and seventy-five cents."

"Okay," Ms. Ruby said. "She must be really special. You see anything you might like?"

"What about that picture frame?" I said. "Aunt Carolyn loves elephants."

"That one kinda **expensive**," she said. "It cost twenty-seven dollars."

I put on my best smile and told her I was a little short.

"You short for true," she said, and chuckled. "If you did have a likkle more money, I woulda sell it to you. But sorry, m'love. The money too short. You see a next one that you like?"

I looked around but didn't see anything else.

"No, thank you," I said. I left Ms. Ruby's feeling a little down.

As I left the store, I saw Uncle Charles walking toward me. I tried to hide, but he had already spotted me.

"Where have you been, Steven?" Uncle Charles asked. "It's almost time for the block party."

Uncle Charles knew how to fix all sorts of things, but he wouldn't do anything unless you paid him. Not even for kids. He was my last chance, though.

"I've been looking for a present for Aunt Carolyn," I explained. "Ms. Ruby's shop is too expensive, and there's nothing special enough at Perkins's."

"Come with me," Uncle Charles said. "I've got just the thing. How much money do you have?"

"Ten dollars," I said. I kept the seventy-five cents for myself. I couldn't let him take all my money!

We went to Uncle Charles's house, which was pretty junky. He had some of everything there—bike parts, old toys, magazines, radios, VCRs, you name it.

Uncle Charles started rummaging around his apartment, looking for things that might be useful. Every few minutes he would hold up something weird.

"What about this?" Uncle Charles would ask.

I would shake my head no.

"You've got to give me some help here," Uncle Charles complained after I said no to several things. So I started digging around. All of a sudden, there it was, the perfect thing.

"Look at this!" I said, holding up a big toy train. It needed a lot of fixing up—the paint was peeling off and some of the windows were broken, but I could see it had **potential**. I got busy right away. I had to work fast if I was going to finish in time to meet Aunt Carolyn at the train station.

I arrived at the station just as the train was coming in. A big crowd of people rushed down the stairs toward me. After almost everybody had left the station, I spotted Aunt Carolyn.

"Hey, Steven!" Aunt Carolyn called. She bustled over and plopped down her bags. She gave me a big kiss, and I gave her a nice, big hug.

"How's my little man doing?" Aunt Carolyn said. "Oh! You've gotten so big and handsome. I don't know who's more handsome now, you or Sean."

"Me of course!" I said, and we both just laughed.

"So what do you have there, Steven?" Aunt Carolyn asked, pointing to the **package** under my arm.

"It's a surprise for you," I said as I handed her the package.

Without saying a word, Aunt Carolyn opened her gift. As soon as she got the **wrapping** off, she put the train up to her face and turned it around and around.

"Steven," Aunt Carolyn said, and gave a big laugh. "This is the best present anyone has ever given me!"

When we got back to my block, everyone was so excited to see Aunt Carolyn that they didn't ask where I had been. They surrounded her as if she were a movie star, their voices shouting out from every direction.

"How have you been, Carolyn?" someone called.

"What did you bring me?" joked another.

"Were you really in Alaska?" asked Sean.

Instead of answering them, Aunt Carolyn held up the train. "Isn't this the most wonderful thing you've ever seen?" she said.

Eagerly they passed around the train, and everyone took real long, careful looks. Sometimes people laughed or made comments.

"Yeah," said Uncle Charles. "That sure is Grandma, always on the phone."

"Look at the Afros on Uncle Charles and Aunt Marsha!" Grandma said, rolling her eyes.

"The Jones Family Express, that sure is right!" said Granddad, chuckling.

Everyone liked the train, even Sean, who made a face and said I should have chosen a better picture of him.

The rest of the day flew by. Aunt Carolyn put her train on an old cake stand in the kitchen window where everyone could see it.

Granddad cooked his best batch of barbecue ever. There were so many greasy barbecue-stained little kids running around that it looked as if they had been in a mud fight. Sean actually won the rap contest. The band liked him so much, they let him be a special guest DJ until it was time to pack up the music. The most surprising thing of all was that Uncle Charles bought ice cream for everybody with my ten dollars and didn't try to eat anyone else's but his own.

STRATEGY SKILL

Make Inferences
Why do you think Uncle Charles bought ice cream for everyone?

Aunt Carolyn sat next to me on the stoop as the whole family told stories, played games, and fought over the last bit of food.

"Steven, thank you for making me feel so special," Aunt Carolyn said. She gave me a little hug and handed me a postcard.

I turned over the postcard and read the message aloud. "Good for one trip with Aunt Carolyn."

I couldn't believe my eyes. I was finally old enough to travel with Aunt Carolyn! Who would have guessed that at the end of the day, I would get the best present of all.

A Postcard From Javaka Steptoe

Javaka Steptoe got the idea for this story from his grandmother. She had an operation and could not go out. Javaka asked a traveling friend to send her postcards from different places to make her feel better. Javaka often uses experiences from his own life in his books. He especially likes to write and illustrate stories about families. He wants readers to open his books and find something that reminds them of their own families.

Other books by Javaka Steptoe:
Hot Day on Abbott Avenue and
In Daddy's Arms I Am Tall

 LOG ON Find out more about Javaka Steptoe at **www.macmillanmh.com**

Write About It

Families are very important to Steven and author Javaka Steptoe. Describe why your family is important to you.

Comprehension Check

Summarize

Summarize the plot of *The Jones Family Express.* Use your Inference Chart to tell about Aunt Carolyn's personality.

Clues	Inference

Think and Compare

1. How do you think Steven and Aunt Carolyn feel about each other? How can you tell? Use your Inference Chart to gather clues. **Visualize: Make Inferences**

2. Reread page 374 of *The Jones Family Express*. What makes Steven's train more special than an ordinary picture of a train? Use story details in your answer. **Evaluate**

3. Would you enjoy traveling with Aunt Carolyn? Explain your answer. **Apply**

4. Why do you think some people would enjoy a personally handmade present more than an **expensive** store-bought present? **Evaluate**

5. Read "My Winter Vacation" on pages 354–355. How does the journal writer seem to feel about her family? How does it compare to the way Steven feels about his family? Use details from both selections in your answer.
Reading/Writing Across Texts

TIPS FOR TRIPS

by Lauren Eckler

Do you want to take the best trip ever? Then you have to plan. Good trips become great trips when you remember one important rule: be prepared.

Packing

Start several days before you leave, so you have time to think of everything you'll need. Make a list of things you want to bring and check items off as you pack. Don't forget to bring directions as well as **identification** that shows your name and home address or phone number.

Preparing

Read about where you are going. Find library books on your **destination** or type the name of the place into an Internet search engine. Add words about your interests, such as "water park" or "whale watching," to find things you would like to do.

Reading Directions

Read these numbered driving directions in order. The distances tell how long to stay on each road.

Directions	**Distance**
1. Turn RIGHT out of HAPPY HOTEL.	0.6 miles
2. Turn LEFT onto KNOTT AVENUE.	0.5 miles
3. Turn RIGHT onto LINCOLN AVENUE.	5.1 miles
4. Turn RIGHT onto EAST WARDLOW ROAD.	1.8 miles
5. End at FLYHIGH AIRPORT.	

TRIP TIME: About 16 minutes   **TOTAL DISTANCE: 8.0 miles**

Read directions to the driver one step at a time. Include the distances. For example, say: "Go 0.6 miles. Then turn left onto Knott Avenue."

Connect and Compare

1 Look at the driving directions. What does the driver do first? How long should the trip take? **Reading Directions**

2. What do you think is the best advice in this article? Explain your answer. **Evaluate**

3. Think about this article and *The Jones Family Express*. How do you think Aunt Carolyn prepares for her trips? **Reading/Writing Across Texts**

Social Studies Activity

Create packing directions for kids to follow for a fun trip. Include tips on the best travel games and emergency supplies.

 Find out more about travel at **www.macmillanmh.com**

Write a Dialogue

Conventions

Writers use dialogue to show what characters are saying. Quotation marks are used around dialogue. If there are more words in the sentence after the dialogue, the dialogue often ends with a comma.

I made up characters in a family. Then I wrote realistic dialogue for them.

I punctuated my dialogue correctly. I used quotation marks around the characters' words.

Surprise, Surprise!

by Vincent L.

Joseph and Francine were planning a surprise party for their mother.

"She will be back in an hour," said Joseph, looking worried.

"Relax," Francine replied. "The cake is on the table. The sign and balloons are up, and everyone will be here soon."

Just then, they heard a knock. "Great. They are here!" Joseph shouted. He ran to the door. "Oh, no!"

It was their mother. "I forgot my key," she said, looking around at the party scene. "Well, this is a surprise!"

382

Your Turn

Write a dialogue between characters in a family. Be sure to use quotation marks and commas correctly. Use the Writer's Checklist to check your writing.

Writer's Checklist

✓ **Ideas and Content:** Is the dialogue believable?

✓ **Organization:** Does the order of the conversation make sense?

✓ **Voice:** Are these characters interesting?

✓ **Word Choice:** Did I choose words that these characters would really use?

✓ **Sentence Fluency:** Do my characters speak the way real people do?

☐ **Conventions:** Did I use quotation marks and commas correctly? Did I use the right tense for each verb? Did I check my spelling?

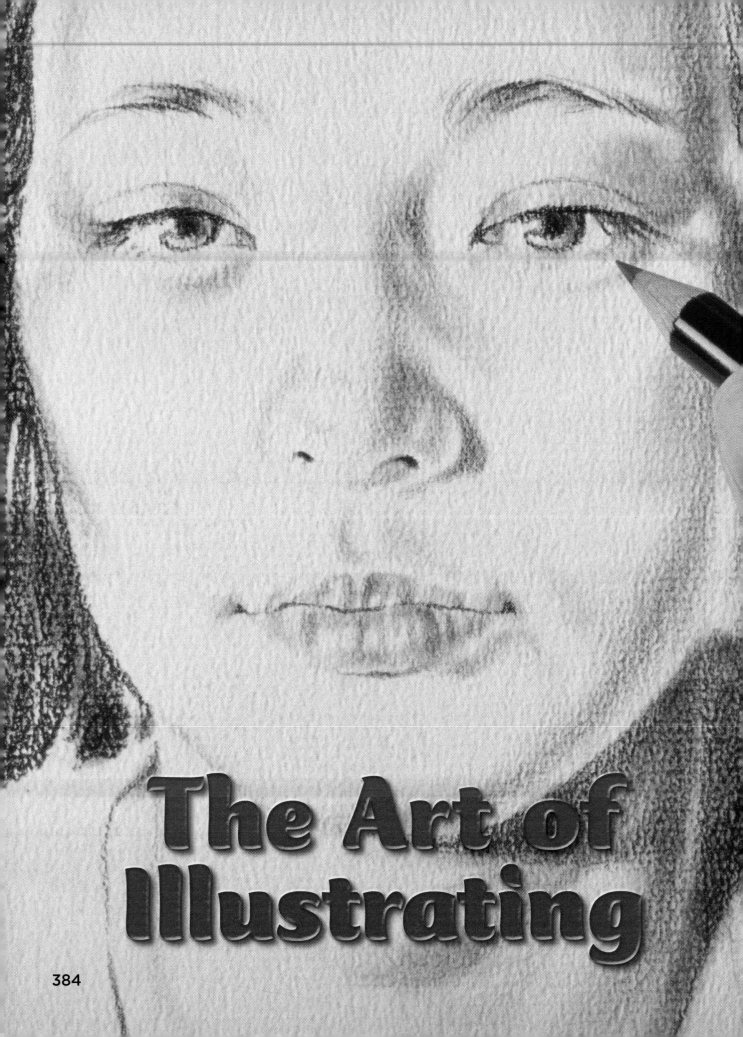

The Art of Illustrating

Talk About It

Illustrations can tell a story without words. What are some things you have illustrated?

LOG ON Find out more about illustrating at **www.macmillanmh.com**

Cave painting found in Lascaux, France

DRAW!

by Jesse Howes

Artists draw on different types of materials. For **instance**, artists have used walls, paper and computer.

CAVE DRAWINGS

The first paintings of horses and other animals were found on cave walls. Scientists think they were made 30,000 years ago.

Why did people **illustrate** cave walls? Before there was paper, artists used what they had—rock!

DRAWING ON PAPER

Paper was invented about 2,000 years ago. Depending on what it's made of, paper can have a unique **style** with different colors and **textures**. It can be plain white or a pattern of different colors, and smooth or bumpy. Plus, it's easier to carry than cave walls!

ANIMATION

About 100 years ago, artists used flipbooks to make moving pictures. Flipbooks have **sketches** placed one on top of the other. Each sketch is a bit different. When the pages are flipped, the drawings seem to move. Next, a camera was used to take pictures of the drawings to make a film.

Today, some artists use computers to draw. They can even draw special effects for video games. Illustration has come a long way in 30,000 years!

TRY IT YOURSELF

Need **suggestions** on what to do in your free time? Make a flipbook. Then, record the pages being flipped on camera, so you can watch it like a movie.

Reread for **Comprehension**

STRATEGY SKILL

Analyze Text Structure
Sequence

Some articles are organized in time order. Clue words that show events in sequence, such as *first, next, then, after that, finally, later, today,* and *at the same time,* can help you analyze the text structure.

A Sequence Chart helps you identify sequence by placing events or actions in the order that they take place. Reread the selection to find the sequence of events.

Event
↓
↓
↓

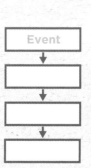

Comprehension

Genre

Narrative Nonfiction is a story about actual events, living things, or people.

Analyze Text Structure

Sequence

As you read, use your Sequence Chart.

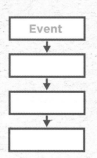

```
Event
  ↓
[        ]
  ↓
[        ]
  ↓
[        ]
```

Read to Find Out

How do illustrators decide what art to create for a book?

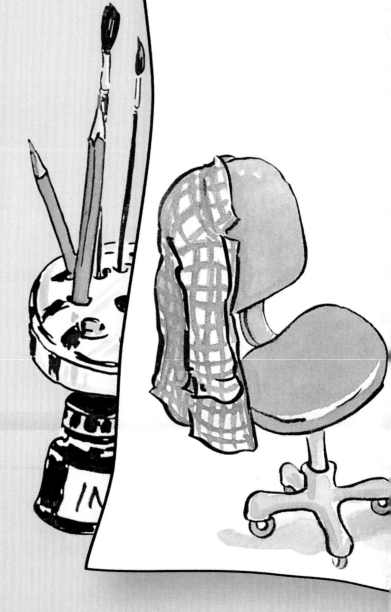

What Do Illustrators Do?

written and illustrated by

EILEEN CHRISTELOW

Award Winning
Author
and
Illustrator

What do illustrators do? They tell stories with pictures.

This picture shows where two illustrators live and work.

Suppose those two illustrators each decided to **illustrate** *Jack and the Beanstalk*. Would they tell the story the same way? Would they draw the same kind of pictures?

I'm going to retell and illustrate JACK AND THE BEANSTALK. *Go lie down, Scooter! I'll take you for a walk later.*

I've been asked to illustrate JACK AND THE BEANSTALK. *Go away, Leonard!*

First, illustrators decide which scenes in the story they want to illustrate …

A plan shows which pictures go on which pages.

After illustrators make a plan for their book, they need to make a dummy. (A dummy is a model of the book.) First they decide what shape and size the book will be.

Then they make **sketches** of the pictures that will go on each page of the dummy.

The first sketches are often rough scribbles on tracing paper.

Sequence
What do illustrators do first?
What do they do next?

As they are sketching, illustrators need to decide how things will look: the characters, their clothes, the setting.

Illustrators can use their imaginations or they may have to do some research.

Some illustrators are also authors. They can change their story as they work on the sketches.

Each illustration has a different problem. For **instance**: From what point of view do you draw the magic bean being planted?

How do you draw a beanstalk so it looks like it's growing?

There is usually more than one way to solve the same problem.

Here is another problem: How do
you make a beanstalk look really TALL?

If the giant doesn't look BIG enough or SCARY enough, the illustrator will draw that picture again.

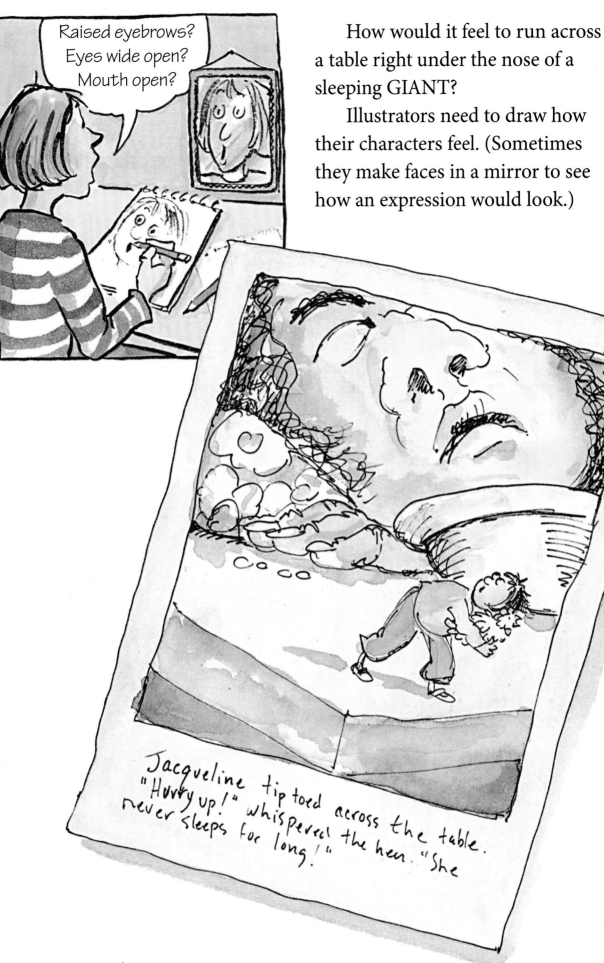

How would it feel to run across a table right under the nose of a sleeping GIANT?

Illustrators need to draw how their characters feel. (Sometimes they make faces in a mirror to see how an expression would look.)

Sometimes illustrators need someone else to model for them.

401

Each illustrator has a different **style** of drawing, just as every person has a different style of handwriting.

We're trying a new style.

The giant . . . Big BOB

Jack . . . Jack Trumper

Jack's mom . . . Ethel Trumper

Jacqueline . . . Jacqueline

Different styles for drawing Jack and Jacqueline

When illustrators have finished their dummies, they show them to the editor and the designer at the publishing company.

The editor decides whether the pictures tell the story.

The designer makes **suggestions** about the design of the book.

She chooses the typeface for the words and the cover.

Sequence
What happens after the dummy is finished?

Illustrators need to decide how they want to do the finished illustrations.

They can draw different kinds of lines and **textures** with different kinds of tools.

pencil

brush

pen with flexible point

felt tip pen

They can color their illustrations with paint, pastels, pencils, or crayons …

They can do an illustration without any black line at all!

watercolors

watercolor crayons

colored pencils

Illustrators need to choose the paper they want to use for their finished illustrations.

Some papers are good for watercolor, others for pastel, others for pencil ... Some are smooth. Some are textured.

Sometimes illustrators throw away their pictures and start again.

Sometimes they change the colors.

Or they may change the composition.

It can take months to finish all the illustrations for a picture book.

Before they are sent to the publisher, they need to be checked to make sure nothing is left out.

Illustrators often do the cover of the book last. The cover tells a lot about a story: What is it about? Does it look interesting?

The cover is a clue to how the illustrator will tell the story.

Would these covers make you want to read the books?

What Does Eileen Christelow Do?

Eileen Christelow had a very strange dream when she was just three years old. She dreamed she could read! In first grade, she really did learn to read. From then on, Eileen's nose was almost always in a book.

As Eileen grew up, she discovered art and photography. She liked to look at children's books and thought about writing and illustrating her own. After a lot of hard work, Eileen's first book was published. Eileen gets her story ideas from newspapers, the radio, and even conversations.

Other books by Eileen Christelow: *Five Little Monkeys Jumping on the Bed* and *What Do Authors Do?*

 LOG ON Find out more about Eileen Christelow at **www.macmillanmh.com**

Write About It

Author Eileen Christelow and the illustrators in her story find story and art ideas in many different places. Describe how you come up with ideas for your stories and art.

Comprehension Check

Summarize

STRATEGY SKILL

Use your Sequence Chart to help you summarize *What Do Illustrators Do?* Tell the steps of illustrating a book in the correct order.

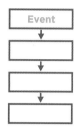

Event

Think and Compare

STRATEGY SKILL

1. What happens just before an illustrator makes dummy **sketches**? **Analyze Text Structure: Sequence**

2. Reread page 393 of *What Do Illustrators Do?* What is the main difference between an illustrator and an illustrator who is also an author? **Analyze**

3. Which illustrator's book would you enjoy more: the traditional story or the version that stars Jacqueline? Give reasons for your answer. **Evaluate**

4. How would you apply what you have learned to illustrate your own story? Explain your answer. **Apply**

5. Read "Draw!" on pages 386–387. How is the way it's written similar to *What Do Illustrators Do?* How are the two stories different? Use details from both selections in your answer. **Reading/Writing Across Texts**

What Does Eileen Do?

She Illustrates!

Jobs in Animation

by Lisa Soo

Animators are artists. Their drawings seem to come to life because the characters move in their animation. Once upon a time, animators only worked on movies. They drew pictures on cards that were flipped in front of the camera to make the characters move. Then computers came along. This new **technology** helps animators draw, color, and move their creations better than ever before!

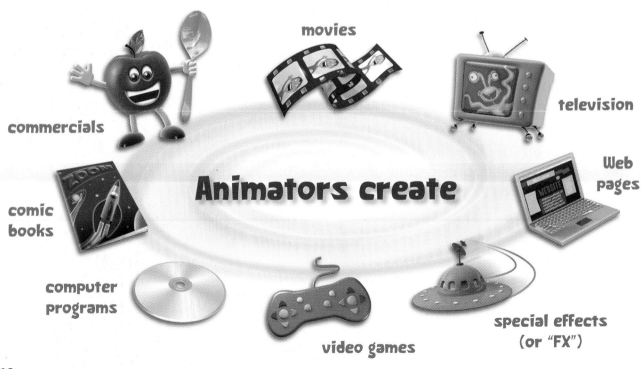

commercials

movies

television

Animators create

comic books

Web pages

computer programs

video games

special effects (or "FX")

412

Today some animators still draw by hand. It takes thousands of drawings to make an animated film this way. There's a lot more to animating than just drawing. It takes a whole team to get the job done. There are people who write the story and people who draw. Others fill in color or add sound.

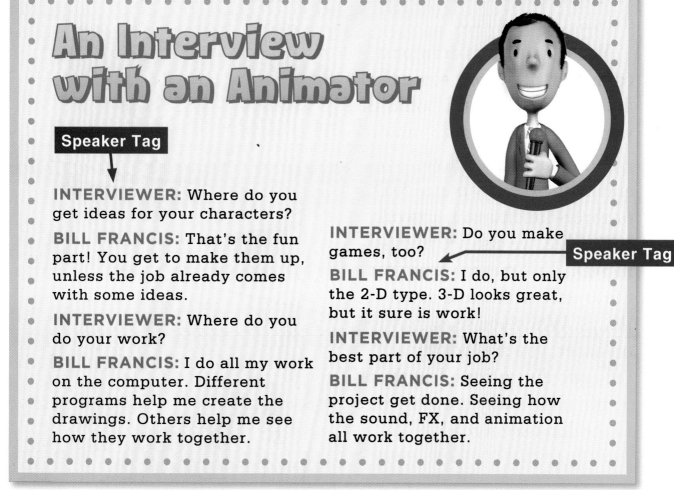

Reading an Interview

SKILL ✓

An interview is a written record of a conversation. Speaker tags show who is talking.

An Interview with an Animator

Speaker Tag

INTERVIEWER: Where do you get ideas for your characters?

BILL FRANCIS: That's the fun part! You get to make them up, unless the job already comes with some ideas.

INTERVIEWER: Where do you do your work?

BILL FRANCIS: I do all my work on the computer. Different programs help me create the drawings. Others help me see how they work together.

INTERVIEWER: Do you make games, too?

Speaker Tag

BILL FRANCIS: I do, but only the 2-D type. 3-D looks great, but it sure is work!

INTERVIEWER: What's the best part of your job?

BILL FRANCIS: Seeing the project get done. Seeing how the sound, FX, and animation all work together.

Telling the Story

It all starts with a story. A director usually comes up with an idea. Then a writer writes a **script**. This tells how the characters, settings, and events take shape. Next comes the **storyboard**. An artist draws the story and puts the pictures up on large boards. Then the writer puts the words with the pictures.

Drawing and Coloring

Animators draw the characters. They also draw any important moving objects. Some animators have helpers who draw tiny details like snowflakes.

When animators draw on a computer, they use a tool called a wand. The animator points the wand at the screen and "draws."

Computers also allow animators to easily create **3-D**, or three-dimensional, artwork. In real life, we also see things in 3-D. That means we can see the length, width, and depth of things. When you see a drawing on paper, you are looking at only two dimensions: length and width. That's why drawings on paper don't seem real!

The 3 Dimensions

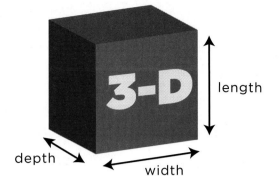

Background Artists

Some artists draw only the story's setting, or background art. Others work only on the colors. They review the colors animators have used, and they make sure the same shades of colors are used so each picture matches the others.

Finishing the Job

The sound team hires actors to be the voices for the characters. The actors read from the scripts. Their voices are recorded and replayed to match the animated pictures. Other members of the sound team add sound effects, such as ringing bells and music.

The drawings, color, story, voices, and music come together in the end to make an animated film. Whether it's a half-hour cartoon or a feature-length movie, you can be sure that a lot of people worked hard to get it to your screen.

Connect and Compare

1. Reread the interview on page 413. Name three things you learned about Bill Francis's job. **Reading an Interview**

2. Based on what you read, what would you enjoy about being an animator? **Evaluate**

3. Think about *What Do Illustrators Do?* and this article. How are the jobs of illustrator and animator alike? How are they different? **Reading/Writing Across Texts**

Fine Arts Activity

Think about an idea for a cartoon character. Draw it on paper or on a computer. Make sure to give your character a name.

 Find out more about animation at **www.macmillanmh.com**

Writing

Word Choice

When you write a play scene, choose words your characters would really use. Think about what your characters are like and where and when they live before you choose their words.

I wrote a play scene for the fairy tale "Rumpelstiltskin."

I chose words that fairy tale characters from long ago would say.

The Miller's Daughter

by Kim R.

Rumpelstiltskin finds the miller's daughter crying in a room full of straw.

Little Man: Why are you sitting and crying at your spinning wheel?

Girl: My father told the King I can spin straw into gold, but I do not know how.

Little Man: Goodness me! What did the King say, my dear?

Girl: I must do it by sunrise, or he will put my father in jail.

Little Man: I can help. What will you give me?

Girl: I'll give you my necklace.

Your Turn

Choose a fairy tale character with a career or talent, and write a play scene. Write one or two sentences that tell where the scene takes place. Then write the name of each speaker followed by the speaker's words. Be sure to choose words that fit your characters and are right for a fairy tale. Use the Writer's Checklist to check your writing.

Writer's Checklist

✓ **Ideas and Content:** Did I choose an interesting part of the story for my scene?

✓ **Organization:** Did I briefly set the scene?

✓ **Voice:** Does my interest in this scene show?

 Word Choice: Did I choose words that fit the characters?

✓ **Sentence Fluency:** Do the characters' words sound good when I read them out loud?

✓ **Conventions:** Did I use colons after the speakers' names? Did I use compound verbs to combine sentences? Did I check my spelling?

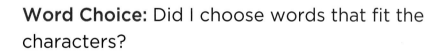

Test Strategy

Right There
The answer is right there on the page. Skim for clues to find the answer.

Design Your Own Journal

by Samantha Gray

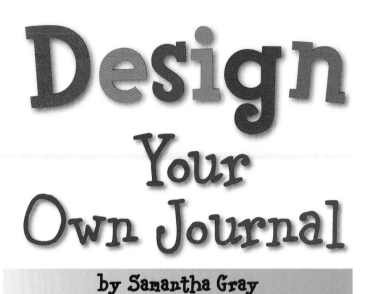

Journal writing can be a lot of fun. You can write about your feelings and things that are important to you. You can describe interesting, happy, and even sad experiences. Your journal will be filled with memories that you can read again and again.

To make your journal special, design it yourself! Here are some directions for making your own journal and the covers that will protect it. Follow the steps in order. Soon, you'll have a journal that's made by you and tells all about you.

Go On ▶

What You'll Need

- 10–15 sheets of white or colored paper
- two pieces of thin cardboard
- ruler
- scissors
- glue

- binder clips
- stapler
- markers, crayons, paints, colored pencils
- decorations, such as shells, yarn, stickers, and photos

Make Your Journal Covers

1 Place a sheet of paper on each piece of cardboard.

2 With a pencil, trace straight lines around the paper's edges.

3 Cut along the lines. These pieces of cardboard will become the covers of your journal.

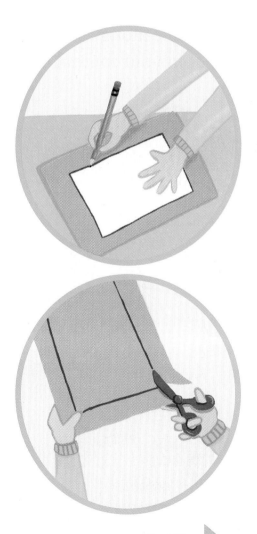

Bind Your Journal

4 With a pencil, draw a faint, vertical line along the left edge of the cover.

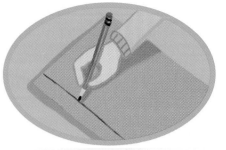

5 Stack the paper for the journal pages between the two cardboard covers. Use binder clips to hold the papers together neatly.

6 Staple along the pencil line. This will hold your journal together.

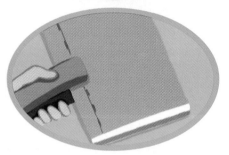

Decorate Your Journal

7 Now it's time to be creative! Decorate the front and back covers of your journal. Use markers, crayons, paints, or colored pencils to add pictures or words to your covers. You could also glue on shells, yarn, stickers, or photos. Choose decorations that are special to you. Now your journal is ready.

Go On ▶

Directions: Answer the questions.

Tip

Skim for clues.

1. The directions say to draw a faint line on the cover. What is the purpose of this line?

   A to show you where your name goes
   B to show you where to glue
   C to show you where to staple
   D to show you where to decorate

2. What is the first thing to do when making a journal?

   A Decorate the journal cover.
   B Paint the cardboard for the covers.
   C Make the journal covers.
   D Bind the journal pages and covers.

3. What is the BEST reason for making a cardboard cover?

   A to protect your journal
   B to hold the staples
   C to practice cutting
   D to win a prize

4. Why do you think it is important to choose decorations that are special to you?

5. Why are there headings in the directions? Why are there pictures? Use examples to support your answers.

Writing Prompt
Think about something that happened this week. Write a one- or two-paragraph journal entry describing your experience. Include details to explain what happened and how it made you feel.

STOP 421

Glossary

What Is a Glossary?

A Glossary can help you find the **meanings** of words in this book that you may not know. The words in the Glossary are listed in **alphabetical order**. **Guide words** at the top of each page tell you the first and last words on the page.

Each word is divided into syllables. The way to pronounce the word is given next. You can understand the pronunciation respelling by using the **pronunciation key**. A shorter key appears at the bottom of every other page. When a word has more than one syllable, a dark accent mark (´) shows which syllable is stressed. In some words, a light accent mark (´) shows which syllable has a less heavy stress. Sometimes an entry includes a second meaning for the word.

Guide Words

First word on the page   Last word on the page

Sample Entry

Pronunciation   Part of Speech

Main entry &
Syllable division

sketch•es (skech´əz) *plural noun.*
Simple drawings that are done ——— Definition
quickly. *I made several **sketches***
Example sentence ——— *before finally painting the tree.*

Pronunciation Key

Phonetic Spelling	Examples	Phonetic Spelling	Examples
a	at, bad, plaid, laugh	d	dear, soda, bad
ā	ape, pain, day, break	f	five, defend, leaf, off, cough, elephant
ä	father, calm		
âr	care, pair, bear, their, where	g	game, ago, fog, egg
e	end, pet, said, heaven, friend	h	hat, ahead
ē	equal, me, feet, team, piece, key	hw	white, whether, which
i	it, big, give, hymn	j	joke, enjoy, gem, page, edge
ī	ice, fine, lie, my	k	kite, bakery, seek, tack, cat
îr	ear, deer, here, pierce	l	lid, sailor, feel, ball, allow
o	odd, hot, watch	m	man, family, dream
ō	old, oat, toe, low	n	not, final, pan, knife, gnaw
ô	coffee, all, taught, law, fought	ng	long, singer
ôr	order, fork, horse, story, pour	p	pail, repair, soap, happy
oi	oil, toy	r	ride, parent, wear, more, marry
ou	out, now, bough	s	sit, aside, pets, cent, pass
u	up, mud, love, double	sh	shoe, washer, fish, mission, nation
ū	use, mule, cue, feud, few	t	tag, pretend, fat, dressed
ü	rule, true, food, fruit	th	thin, panther, both
u̇	put, wood, should, look	th	these, mother, smooth
ûr	burn, hurry, term, bird, word, courage	v	very, favor, wave
		w	wet, weather, reward
ə	about, taken, pencil, lemon, circus	y	yes, onion
b	bat, above, job	z	zoo, lazy, jazz, rose, dogs, houses
ch	chin, such, match	zh	vision, treasure, seizure

Aa

ac·cept·ance (ak sep′təns) *noun.* An agreement to take something given or offered. *My sister learned of her* **acceptance** *to college yesterday.*

ached (ākt) *verb.* Had a dull and steady pain. *Hannah's tooth* **ached** *all day, so she went to the dentist.*

ad·dress·ing (ə dres′ing) *verb.* Tackling a problem. *While she was* **addressing** *her homework, Tiffany heard that school was cancelled.*

ad·mire (ad mīr′) *verb.* To respect or think well of someone or something. *The team had to* **admire** *the coach for never giving up.*

a·do·be (ə dō′bē) *adjective.* Brick made of clay and straw and dried in the sun. *Some people in the southwestern United States live in* **adobe** *houses.*

ad·vised (ad vīzd′) *verb.* Offered ideas about solving a problem. *The dentist* **advised** *me to brush more often to prevent cavities.*

a·gree·a·ble (ə grē′ə bəl) *adjective.* Nice; pleasant. *The flowers in the room had an* **agreeable** *smell.*

aisles (īlz) *plural noun.* The space between rows of seats or rows of shelves at a store. *My teacher asks us to keep the* **aisles** *free of backpacks.*

an·i·ma·tors (an′ə mā′tərz) *plural noun.* Artists or technicians who draw and produce cartoons. *Many* **animators** *today use computers to bring their drawings to life.*

an·nounced (ə nounst′) *verb.* Told something in a loud or official way. *The winners of the writing contest were* **announced** *at the assembly.*

an·nu·al (an′ū əl) *adjective.* Happening once a year. *Every July 4, my family holds an* **annual** *family reunion.*

ap·pe·tite (ap′i tīt′) *noun.* A desire for food. *On the first day of school, I usually have no* **appetite** *for breakfast.*

at·tracts (ə trakts´) *verb.* Draws or pulls, either by physical force or by gaining the attention or admiration of. *Because of his loud laugh, Jaime always* **attracts** *the attention of strangers.*

Bb

ban·quet (bang´kwit) *noun.* A large meal presented for an important event or date. *My soccer team has a* **banquet** *at the end of the season.*

Word History

Banquet comes from the Old French word *banc,* meaning "little bench." From there, it progressed to "meal taken on the family workbench" and then it became "feast."

both·er·ing (both´ər ing) *verb.* **1.** Giving someone trouble or annoying them. *Henry's need to talk while watching TV was* **bothering** *Maria.* **2.** Taking the time to do something. *My dad said no without even* **bothering** *to look up from the paper.*

bright·ness (brīt´nes) *noun.* The amount of light given off by something. *The* **brightness** *of certain stars depends partly on how far they are from Earth.*

Cc

chal·lenge (chal´ənj) *noun.* Something calling for work, effort, and the use of one's talents. *The math problem was a* **challenge**, *but Jan found the answer.*

cha·pa·tis (chə pä´tēz) *plural noun.* Flat, disk-shaped bread made in northern India. *It was the first time she'd eaten* **chapatis**, *but right away she knew she liked them.*

at; āpe; fär; câre; end; mē; it; īce; pîerce; hot; ōld; sông; fôrk; oil; out; up; ūse; rüle; pu̇ll; tûrn; chin; sing; shop; thin; this; hw in white; zh in treasure.

The symbol ə stands for the unstressed vowel sound in about, taken, pencil, lemon, and circus.

chuck·led (chuk´əld) *verb.* Laughed in a quiet way. *When the plan worked, Calvin **chuckled** to himself.*

com·mu·ni·cate (kə myū´ni kāt´) *verb.* To pass along or exchange information, thoughts, or ideas. *It is difficult to **communicate** with people who do not listen.*

com·put·er (kəm pū´tər) *noun.* An electronic device which stores and processes large amounts of information and is able to perform complicated mathematical tasks. *He used his sister's **computer** to look for information on the Internet.*

Word History

Computer comes from the Latin *com-,* which means "with," and *putare,* "to reckon." It first meant a person who works with numbers.

con·cen·trate (kon´sən trāt´) *verb.* Pay attention or think very carefully about something being done. *If the TV is on, I find it hard to **concentrate** on anything else.*

con·tent (kən tent´) *adjective.* Satisfied, happy. *The tables at the party were filled with food, but she was **content** with just a snack.*

con·ver·sa·tion (kon´vər sā´shən) *noun.* A talk between two or more people. *He always enjoyed their **conversation** whenever she came to visit.*

crack·le (krak´əl) *verb.* To make a series of small, sharp snapping noises. *I like to hear the wood **crackle** in the fireplace.*

cu·ri·os·i·ty (kyûr´ē os´i tē) *noun.* An interesting or strange thing. *A typewriter is a **curiosity** in a world of computers.*

Dd

dan·ger·ous (dān´jər əs) *adjective.* Likely to cause harm; unsafe. *Playing in the street is **dangerous**.*

dark·ened (där´kənd) *adjective.* Made or became darker or blacker, so there is less light. *The **darkened** room looked scary.*

dec·o·rat·ed (dek´ə rāt´əd) *adjective.* Made to look better by adding pretty things to it. *The table was **decorated** with colorful flowers.*

den (den) *noun.* **1.** A place, often underground or in a cave, where wild animals live. *The bears crawl into their **den** each winter for a long sleep.* **2.** A small, cozy room for reading or studying. *Jane studies at her computer in the **den**.*

de·part (di pärt′) *verb.* Leave or go away. *The bus will **depart** at 7:00 A.M.*

des·tin·a·tion (des′tə nā′shən) *noun.* The place to which one is going. *They had already walked three miles, but their **destination** was still far ahead.*

dim (dim) *adjective.* Having or giving little light; not bright. *Once the sun had set, the room grew too **dim** for reading.*

dis·cour·aged (dis kûr′ijd) *adjective.* Having little or no hope. *Brad felt **discouraged** after losing the first race.*

down¹ (doun) *noun.* Fine, soft feathers. *During cold winter nights, the best way to stay warm is under a quilt filled with **down**.*

down² (doun) *adverb.* From a higher to a lower place. *The boy's mother told him to get **down** from the tree.*

down·stairs (doun′stârz′) *adjective.* Down the stairs; on or to a lower floor. *The kitchen is **downstairs**, and the bedrooms are upstairs.*

Ee

eas·i·ly (ē′zə lē) *adverb.* Without problems or difficulties. *Heather studied her spelling words, so she **easily** got a perfect score on her quiz.*

at; āpe; fär; câre; end; mē; it; īce; pîerce; hot; ōld; sông; fôrk; oil; out; up; ūse; rüle; pùll; tûrn; chin; sing; shop; thin; this; hw in white; zh in treasure.

The symbol ə stands for the unstressed vowel sound in about, taken, pencil, lemon, and circus.

ech·oes (ek´ōz) *verb.* Repeats a sound. *I can hear the bird's screech as it* **echoes** *across the valley.*

Word History

In Greek mythology, Echo was a beautiful maiden whose longtime love for Narcissus caused her body to weaken so much that only her voice remained.

en·ter·tain·ment (en´tər tān´mənt) *noun.* Something that pleases, amuses or interests, especially a performance or show. *His favorite type of* **entertainment** *was going to the movies.*

en·ve·lope (en´və lōp´ or än´və lōp´) *noun.* A flat paper container often used for sending letters through the mail. *Put the letter in the* **envelope** *and write the address on the front.*

ex·cite·ment (ek sīt´mənt) *noun.* A feeling of being happy because something good has happened or will happen. *The class was full of* **excitement** *before the show began.*

ex·pen·sive (ek spen´siv) *adjective.* Costing a lot of money. *A wonderful gift does not have to be* **expensive**.

Ff

far·ther (fär´thər) *adverb.* At a greater distance than something else. *The mountains were* **farther** *away than the river.*

far·thest (fär´thist) *adverb.* At the greatest distance away. *Maria lives* **farthest** *away from school.*

fierce (fîrs) *adjective.* Very strong or violent. *The* **fierce** *hurricane affected the whole state.*

fum·bled (fum´bəld) *verb.* Tried to get hold of or handled in a clumsy way. *I* **fumbled** *around in the dark for my glasses.*

Gg

gaze (gāz) *verb.* To look at for a long time. *I like to* **gaze** *at the ocean because the waves make me calm.* *noun.* A long, steady look or stare. *Her curious* **gaze** *made him wonder if they knew each other.*

gnaws (nôz) *verb.* Bites something hard again and again in order to wear away little by little. *My dog **gnaws** on bones all day.*

guests (gests) *plural noun.* People who come to visit or eat a meal. *The **guests** arrived for the party just before dinner.*

Hh

health·y (hel′thē) *adjective.* Having, showing, or giving good health. *A **healthy** diet includes fruits and vegetables.*

heart·y (här′tē) *adjective.* **1.** Full of warmth, kindness, or enthusiasm. *They greeted her with a **hearty** welcome.* **2.** Big and satisfying. *It was the kind of **hearty** meal he expected after an hour of shoveling snow.*

home page (hōm′pāj) *noun.* The opening or main page of a Web site. *Her **home page** was filled with pictures from her latest trip.*

hud·dle (hud′əl) *noun.* A group of people or animals close together. *The puppies were cold so they snuggled together in a **huddle**. verb.* To gather close together in a bunch. *During the winter fire drill, the students had to **huddle** up to keep warm.*

hy·per·links (hī′pər lingks′) *plural noun.* Highlighted text or graphics on a computer page which, when selected, direct users to a new page. *The Web page contained **hyperlinks** to a wide variety of interesting sites.*

Ii

i·den·ti·fi·ca·tion (ī den′tə fi kā′shən) *noun.* **1.** The act of identifying. *Improper **identification** by the witness meant the suspect would go free.* **2.** Proof or evidence of who a person is. *The video store clerk could not rent the movie to us without proper **identification***.

---

at; āpe; fär; câre; end; mē; it; īce; pîerce; hot; ōld; sông; fôrk; oil; out; up; ūse; rüle; pull; tûrn; chin; sing; shop; thin; this; hw in white; zh in treasure.

The symbol ə stands for the unstressed vowel sound in about, taken, pencil, lemon, and circus.

il·lus·trate (il′ə strāt) *verb.* To draw a picture or diagram to explain or decorate something written. *The art teacher helped me* **illustrate** *my story.*

im·ag·es (im′ij əz) *plural noun.* Drawings, pictures, or other likenesses of persons or things. **Images** *of wildlife were painted across the museum's walls.*

im·proved (im prüvd′) *verb.* Made or became better. *Her drawing ability had greatly* **improved** *since the last time he saw her.*

Word History

Improve is from the Middle English *improwen,* to enclose land for farming, and from Anglo-Norman *emprouwer,* to turn to profit.

in·crease (in krēs′) *verb.* To make bigger or greater. *Each year, we* **increase** *the size of the garden by adding a row of plants.*

in·no·cent (in′ə sənt) *adjective.* Not guilty; harmless. *The puppy looked* **innocent***, but we knew she knocked over the cup.*

in·stance (in′stəns) *noun.* An example. *You might want to go to the park, for* **instance***.*

in·tro·duce (in′trə düs′, -dyüs′) *verb.* To make acquainted or present by name. *The captain always likes to* **introduce** *himself to the ship's guests before the journey begins.*

Jj

jun·ior (jün′yər) *adjective.* The younger or smaller of two. *Ralphie was a* **junior** *version of his father, Clancy.*

Kk

kim·chi (kim′chē) *also* **kim·chee** *noun.* Korean dish made of seasoned vegetables, such as cabbage or radishes, which are then fermented. *Kimchi is one of the most popular dishes in Korea.*

Ll

light-year (līt′yîr′) *noun.* The distance that light travels through space in one year. *A star that is one **light-year** away is about 5,880,000 miles from us!*

main (mān) *adjective.* Most important. *The book I needed was at the library's **main** branch.*

man·age (man′ij) *verb.* To succeed at doing something; be able to. *Mom did **manage** to stop the leak before too much water went onto the floor.*

meas·ure·ment (mezh′ər mənt) *noun.* Something found or shown by measuring. *The builder took a **measurement** of the land around the house.*

men·u (men′ū) *noun.* **1.** A list of all the articles and information on a Web site. *I used the Web site's **menu** to find the information I needed.* **2.** The list of items served at a restaurant. *There were a lot of tasty dishes on the **menu**.*

Nn

neigh·bor·hood (nā′bər hu̇d′) *noun.* A small area or district in a town or city where people live. *Justine and Horatio were surprised to learn that they both lived in the same **neighborhood**.*

---

at; āpe; fär; câre; end; mē; it; īce; pîerce; hot; ōld; sông; fôrk; oil; out; up; ūse; rüle; pu̇ll; tûrn; chin; sing; shop; thin; th̶is; hw in white; zh in treasure.

The symbol ə stands for the unstressed vowel sound in about, taken, pencil, lemon, and circus.

nerv·ous (nûr′vəs) *adjective.* Not able to relax; tense or fearful. *Barking dogs make my aunt **nervous**.*

Word History

Nervous comes from the Latin word *nervosus,* meaning "sinewy" or containing nerves.

non·sense (non′sens) *noun.* Words or actions that are silly and make no sense. *The talk about a monster in the closet was **nonsense**.*

Oo

ob·jects (ob′jikts *for noun;* əb jekts′ *for verb*) *plural noun.* Anything that can be seen and touched; things. *Tracey found a variety of **objects** that had been washed in by the tide. verb.* Presents an opposite argument. *Mr. McNiff **objects** to using garlic in the pasta sauce.*

ob·served (əb zûrvd′) *verb.* Learned by studying someone or something. *The students **observed** the change in temperature over the past three weeks.*

off·spring (ôf′spring′) *noun.* The young of a person, animal, or plant. *A lioness and her three **offspring** approached the waterhole, frightening off the other animals.*

Pp

pack·age (pak′ij) *noun.* Something put in a box, case, or container, or covered in paper. *A **package** arrived in the mail today.*

pas·sion (pash′ən) *noun.* A very strong feeling or liking for something. *Love is a **passion**, and so is anger.*

pass·port (pas′pôrt) *noun.* An official government document that confirms one's identity as a legal citizen and allows for travel to other countries. *Marilyn had to get a **passport** if she wanted to go to Ghana.*

per·fect (pûr′fikt *for adjective;* pər fekt′ *for verb*) *adjective.* Without a fault or mistake. *The weather was **perfect** for a day at the beach. verb.* To bring perfection or completion. *Anita wanted to **perfect** the book's design before it was printed.*

pho·to·graph (fō′tə graf′) *noun.* A picture that is made with a camera. *I've learned to print a **photograph** from a computer.*

po·lite·ly (pə līt′lē) *adverb.* In a way that shows good manners or consideration for others' feelings. *When my friend arrived, he greeted my parents **politely**.*

po·ten·tial (pə ten′shəl) *noun.* Possibility to become something more. *The runners had great **potential**, but they would have to practice more.*

pre·dic·tions (pri dik′shənz) *plural noun.* Attempts at guessing beforehand. *Several **predictions** were made about who would win the science fair.*

pre·serve (pri zûrv′) **1.** *noun.* A piece of land set aside to protect plants and animals. *I donated land to a **preserve** for wild horses.* **2.** *verb.* To keep from changing; to protect. *Neil was able to **preserve** his comic books by keeping them in sealed plastic bags.*

---

at; āpe; fär; câre; end; mē; it; īce; pîerce; hot; ōld; sông; fôrk; oil; out; up; ūse; rüle; pùll; tûrn; chin; sing; shop; thin; this; hw in white; zh in treasure.

The symbol ə stands for the unstressed vowel sound in about, taken, pencil, lemon, and circus.

prob·a·bly (prob′ə blē) *adverb.* Most likely to happen or be true. *Ms. Fine will **probably** come back to work on Wednesday.*

prop·er (prop′ər) *adjective.* Correct or suitable for a certain purpose. *My brother showed me the **proper** way to tie a necktie.*

Rr

rain·fall (rān′fôl′) *noun.* The amount of rain, snow, sleet, or hail that falls on an area in a certain amount of time. *The annual **rainfall** for the town was the highest it had ever been.*

rep·u·ta·tion (rep′yə tā′shən) *noun.* What most people think of a person or thing. *Micheline's **reputation** as a speller has gotten better since she won the spelling bee.*

re·sort (ri zôrt′) *verb.* To use or go to for help. *Lucy didn't want to **resort** to asking for directions. noun.* A place where people go for fun and relaxation. *Joseph wasn't sure if he could afford that **resort** in the Bahamas.*

Word History

The history of **resort** can be traced back through the Middle English word *resorten,* "to return," and the Old French *resortir,* which meant "to go out again."

re·store (ri stôr′) *verb.* To bring back; establish again. *Mrs. Knox wanted to **restore** peace to the neighborhood.*

Ss

sat·is·fy (sat′is fī′) *verb.* To be or give enough to meet a need, desire, or demand. *Joel has to **satisfy** all the requirements to earn a good grade.*

scratch (skrach) *verb.* **1.** To scrape or cut with something sharp, such as nails. *The cat liked to **scratch** the arm of the couch.* **2.** To cancel or strike out. *I was able to **scratch** milk off my grocery list.*

script (skript) *noun.* **1.** The text of a play, movie, or television show. *The **script** wasn't very long, so it would be easy for her to memorize the lines.*
2. A style of writing using cursive characters. *The boy had not learned how to write **script**, so he printed the words instead.*

se·cur·ing (si kyür'ing) *verb.* Attaching or tying something so it doesn't move. *By **securing** the flashlight to the tent pole, he was able to read with both hands.*

shuf·fles (shuf'əlz) *verb.* Walks without lifting the feet off the ground. *My little brother **shuffles** when he doesn't want to leave.*

side·bar (sīd'bär) *noun.* A column at the side of a Web page that has more information. *The story about the baby panda ran as a **sidebar** on the zoo's home page.*

sin·gle (sing'gəl) *adjective.* One. *Not a **single** person knew about the event.*

sketch·es (skech'əz) *plural noun.* Simple drawings that are done quickly. *I made several **sketches** before finally painting the tree.*

soared (sôrd) *verb.* Flew high in the air. *The hawk **soared** above the meadow.*

so·lar sys·tem (sō'lər sis'təm) *noun.* The sun and all the planets, satellites, and comets that circle around it. *Jupiter is the largest planet in our **solar system**.*

splen·did (splen'did) *adjective.* Very good or beautiful. *Some birds have **splendid** feathers of many colors.*

Word History

The word splendid comes from the Latin *splendere*, "to shine."

at; āpe; fär; câre; end; mē; it; īce; pîerce; hot; ōld; sông; fôrk; oil; out; up; ūse; rüle; pull; tûrn; chin; sing; shop; thin; this; hw in white; zh in treasure.

The symbol ə stands for the unstressed vowel sound in about, taken, pencil, lemon, and circus.

star·ry (stä′rē) *adjective.* Full of stars or heavenly bodies that shine by their own light. *The **starry** sky made the nighttime seem bright.*

stem (stem) *noun.* A slender stalk connecting one part of a plant to another, such as a fruit or leaf to a branch. *He always likes to pull out the **stem** before eating an apple. verb.* To make progress against. *The empire, with its larger army, was able to **stem** the rebellion.*

sto·ry·board (stôr′ē bôrd′) *noun.* A series of drawings or sketches that shows how the action of a film or video will be shot. *According to the **storyboard**, there would be a lot of effects in the next scene.*

style (stīl) *noun.* A particular way of saying or doing something. *Every singer has his or her own **style**.*

Word History

A long time ago, the word **style** meant "a pen," which came from the Latin *stylus*, a pointed instrument used for writing.

suf·fered (suf′ərd) *verb.* Felt pain or distress. *Stephen **suffered** from loneliness the first time his brother went off to school.*

sug·ges·tions (səg jes′chənz) *plural noun.* Ideas or plans offered for others to think about. *The artist made **suggestions** for ways to improve Arthur's painting.*

suit·a·ble (sü′tə bəl) *adjective.* Proper or right. *A new paintbrush is a **suitable** gift for my art teacher.*

sym·bol (sim′bəl) *noun.* A picture or shape that stands for something else. *The heart is a* **symbol** *for love.*

Word History

Symbol is derived from the Latin word *symbolum,* meaning "token" or "mark," and the Greek *sumbolon,* which means "token for identification."

Tt

tal·ent·ed (tal′ənt əd) *adjective.* Having a natural ability or skill. *I didn't know Curtis was such a* **talented** *pianist.*

tech·nol·o·gy (tek nol′ə jē) *noun.* **1.** The use of science for practical purposes, especially in engineering and industry. **2.** Methods, machines, and devices that are used in doing things in a science or profession. *With* **technology** *changing every day, it is sometimes difficult to keep up.*

tel·e·scope (tel′ə skōp) *noun.* A tool that makes faraway objects look larger and closer. *Lucia used her new* **telescope** *to get a closer look at the craters on the moon.*

tem·per·a·tures (tem′pər ə choorz′, -chərz, tem′prə-) *plural noun.* Measures of how hot or cold things are. *The* **temperatures** *on the sun are very high.*

tex·tures (teks′chərz) *plural noun.* The way a surface looks or how it feels when you touch it. *Fabrics have many* **textures,** *from silky to rough.*

at; āpe; fär; câre; end; mē; it; īce; pîerce; hot; ōld; sông; fôrk; oil; out; up; ūse; rüle; pull; tûrn; chin; sing; shop; thin; this; hw in white; zh in treasure.

The symbol ə stands for the unstressed vowel sound in about, taken, pencil, lemon, and circus.

3-D (thrē′dē) *adjective.* Three-dimensional. *The images on the computer created the illusion of being **3-D**.*

tor·til·las (tôr tē′yəz) *plural noun.* Thin, round, flat breads made from water and cornmeal or wheat. *They were the best **tortillas** he'd eaten since coming to Mexico.*

Word History

Tortilla is from the Spanish word *torta*, or cake, which in Latin means a kind of bread.

trudged (trujd) *verb.* Walked slowly and with effort. *The children **trudged** up the snowy hill to go sledding.*

Uu

u·nique (ū nēk′) *adjective.* One of a kind, unusual. *Because Tess was from another country, she seemed to have a **unique** way of talking.*

un·trust·ing (un trust′ing) *adjective.* Having doubt about something. *The **untrusting** neighbor did not open his door.*

URL (ū är el′) *noun.* An Internet address, standing for **U**niform **R**esource **L**ocator. *He e-mailed the Web site's **URL** to his friend in Japan.*

use·ful (ūs′fəl) *adjective.* Helpful; serving a good use or purpose. *My mom always tells me to make myself **useful** by helping others.*

Ww

weak·est (wēk′est) *adjective.* Least strong or powerful. *I feel **weakest** in the morning, right before eating breakfast.*

wear·i·ly (wîr′ə lē) *adverb.* Acting very tired. *The bus driver **wearily** returned home after her long day.*

whips (hwips *or* wips) *verb.* Moves or hits quickly and suddenly. *Walking can be hard when the wind **whips** around corners.*

wrap·ping (rap′ing) *noun.* Paper or other material used to cover or protect something. *Aunt Marie likes to see pretty **wrapping** on a present.*

Acknowledgments

The publisher gratefully acknowledges permission to reprint the following copyrighted material:

"A lonely sparrow" by Kazue Mizumura from POEM-MAKING: WAYS TO BEGIN WRITING POETRY by Myra Cohn Livingston. Copyright © 1999 by Myra Cohn Livingston. Reprinted with permission by HarperCollins Children's Books, a division of HarperCollins Publishers.

"Antarctic Anthem" by Judy Sierra, illustrations by Jose Aruego and Ariane Dewey from ANTARCTIC ANTICS by Judy Sierra. Text copyright © 1998 by Judy Sierra. Illustrations copyright © 1998 by Jose Aruego and Ariane Dewey. Reprinted with permission by Gulliver Books, Harcourt Brace and Company.

"Author: A True Story" by Helen Lester. Copyright © 1997 by Helen Lester. Reprinted by permission of Houghton Mifflin Books.

"Broken and broken" by Chosu, translated by Harry Behn, from "Cricket Song: Japanese Haiku Translated" by Harry Behn. Copyright © 1964 by Harry Behn. Copyright renewed © 1992 by Prescott Behn, Pamela Behn Adam, and Peter Behn. Used by permission of Marian Reiner. Compilation and introduction from LIGHT-GATHERING POEMS edited by Liz Rosenberg. Compilation and introduction copyright © 2000 by Liz Rosenberg. Reprinted with permission by Henry Holt and Company, LLC.

"Dear Juno" by Soyung Pak, illustrations by Susan Kathleen Hartung. Text copyright © 1999 by Soyung Pak. Illustrations copyright © 1999 by Susan Kathleen Hartung. Reprinted with permission of Penguin Putnam Books for Young Readers, Penguin Books Ltd.

"First Day Jitters" by Julie Danneberg, illustrations by Judy Love. Text copyright © 2000 by Julie Danneberg. Illustrations copyright © 2000 by Judy Love. Reprinted with permission of Charlesbridge, Charlesbridge Publishing, Inc. All rights reserved.

"The Jones Family Express" by Javaka Steptoe. Text and illustrations copyright © 2003 by Javaka Steptoe. Reprinted by permission of Lee & Low Books, Inc.

"One Riddle, One Answer" by Lauren Thompson, illustrations by Linda S. Wingerter. Text copyright © 2001 by Lauren Thompson. Illustrations copyright © 2001 by Linda S. Wingerter. All rights reserved. Reprinted with permission of Scholastic Press, a division of Scholastic, Inc.

"Penguin Chick" by Betty Tatham, illustrations by Helen K. Davie. Text copyright © 2002 by Betty Tatham. Illustrations copyright © 2002 by Helen K. Davie. Reprinted with permission by HarperCollins Children's Books, a division of HarperCollins Publishers.

"The Perfect Pet" by Margie Palatini, illustrations by Bruce Whatley. Text copyright © 2003 by Margie Palatini. Illustrations copyright © 2003 by Bruce Whatley. Reprinted with permission by HarperCollins Children's Books, a division of HarperCollins Publishers.

"The Planets in Our Solar System" by Franklyn M. Branley, illustrations by Kevin O'Malley. Text copyright ©1981 Franklyn M. Branley. Illustrations copyright ©1998 Kevin O'Malley. Reprinted with permission by Let's Read and Find Out Science, a division of HarperCollins Publishers.

"Shiny colored tents" by Myra Cohn Livingston from CRICKET NEVER DOES by Myra Cohn Livingston. Text copyright © 1997 by Myra Cohn Livingston. Reprinted with permission by Margaret K. McElderry Books, an imprint of Simon & Schuster Children's Publishing Division.

"Stone Soup" by Jon J Muth. Copyright © 2003 by Jon J Muth. Reprinted with permission of Scholastic Press, a division of Scholastic Inc.

"The Strongest One" by Joseph Bruchac from PUSHING UP THE SKY: SEVEN NATIVE AMERICAN PLAYS FOR CHILDREN by Joseph Bruchac. Text copyright © 2000 by Joseph Bruchac. Reprinted with permission by Dial Books for Young Readers, a division of Penguin Putnam Inc.

"What Do Illustrators Do?" by Eileen Christelow. Copyright © 1999 by Eileen Christelow. Reprinted with permission by Clarion Books, an imprint of Houghton Mifflin Company.

"Where I Sit Writing" by Allan Ahlberg from THE MYSTERIES OF ZIGOMAR: POEMS AND STORIES by Allan Ahlberg. Text copyright © 1997 by Allan Ahlberg. Reprinted with permission of Candlewick Press.

"Wolf" by Becky Bloom, illustrations by Pascal Biet. Copyright © 1999 by Siphano, Montpellier. Reprinted with permission by Orchard Books, a Grolier Company.

ILLUSTRATIONS
Cover Illustration: Lisa Falkenstern

14-33: Judy Love. 36: Tim Johnson. 42-67: Susan Kathleen Hartung. 68-71: Wetzel & Company. 72: Tim Johnson. 76: Digital Image At The Museum of Modern Art/Licensed by Scala/Art Resource. 81: Rick Nease for TFK. 90-111: Helen K. Davie. 114: Tim Johnson. 120-139: Bruce Whatley. 140-141: (bkgd) Wetzel & Company. 143: Karen Beckhardt. 148-150: Laura Ovresat. 154-155: Cindy Revell. 156-171: Lucia Angela Perez. 176: Tim Johnson. 180: Jason Abbott. 182-205: Pascal Biet. 210: Tim Johnson. 214: Rick Nease for TFK. 216-219: Don Foley. 218-219: (bkgd) Kevin O'Malley. 220: (tcr) George Toomer. 220-249: Kevin O'Malley. 252: Rob Schuster. 254-255: Tim Johnson. 260-273: Helen Lester. 274-275: Laura Watson. 276: Tim Johnson. 286-307: Jon J Muth. 312: Tim Johnson. 318-335: Linda S. Wingerter. 336-337: Stephanie Langley. 338-339: Tim Johnson. 342: Rick Nease for TFK. 356-379: Javaka Steptoe. 378-379: (bkgd) Wetzel & Company. 382: Tim Johnson. 388-411: Eileen Christelow. 412-415: Chris Boyd. 416: Tim Johnson. 418-420: Cathi Mingus. 422-423: Kathy Ember.

PHOTOGRAPHY
All Photographs are by Macmillan/McGraw Hill (MMH) except as noted below:

10-11: (bkgd) Jose Luis Pelaez/CORBIS. 11: Digital Vision/Punchstock. 12: (tr) Royalty Free/CORBIS; (tc) Don Tremain/Getty Images. 13: David Young-Wolf/Photo Edit Inc. 32: Courtesy Charlesbridge Press. 34: Jim West/The Image Works. 35: Michael Newman/Photo Edit Inc. 36: Royalty-Free/CORBIS. 37: Syracuse Newspapers/C.W. McKeen/The Image Works. 38-39: © Craig Hammell/CORBIS. 39: Ryan McVay/Getty Images. 40: (tr) Steve Cole/Masterfile; (cl) Paul Wenham-Clark/Masterfile; (bl) Jeff Greenberg/The Image Works. 41: (tr) Jeff Greenberg/The Image Works; (r) Photodisc/ Picture Quest. 66: (tcl) Courtesy Soyung Pak; (bcr) Courtesy Susan Kathleen Hartung. 68: (bc) Underwood & Underwood/CORBIS; (br) Leonard de Selva/CORBIS. 69: (cr) J Richards/ Alamy; (bl) Bettmann/ CORBIS;(bc) National Archive/Newsmakers/Getty Images; (br) Roberts H. Armstrong/Robertstock/Retrofile; (cl) Leonard de Selva/CORBIS. 70: (tr) Rubberball Productions/Getty Images; (cl) Photodisc/Getty Images; (br) Myrleen Ferguson Gate/Photo Edit Inc. 71: Stewart Cohen/Stone/Getty Images. 72: Tom Prettyman/ Photo Edit Inc. 73: Silver Editions. 74-75: Kathy McLaughlin /The Image Works. 76: George Rose/Getty Images. 77: (tr) Kelly Kerr; (bl) Paula Bronstein/Getty Images. 78: Gregory Ochocki/Photo Researchers. 79: S. Michael Bisceglie/Animals Animals. 80: (tl) Bill Cooke; (cl) Gary Griffen/Animals Animals; (bl) Nancy Richmond/ The Image Works. 81: (cl) Brian K. Miller/Animals Animals; (c) Don Enger/Animals Animals; (bl) Lightwave Photography/Animals Animals; (bc) Robert Sabin/Animals Animals. 82: Time & Life Pictures/Getty Images. 84: Amos Morgan/Photodisc/Punchstock. 85: (bkgd) Dian Lofton for TFK; (cl) Burke/Triolo Productions/Brand X/Alamy; (cr) Ryan McVay/Getty Images. 86-87: (bkgd) Steve Bloom Images/Alamy. 87: (inset) Photodisc/Getty Images. 88: (cl) A.N.T./ Photo Researchers; (b) PhotoLink/Getty Images. 89: Wolfgang Kaehler/CORBIS. 110: (tc) Image: Alex Lowy/lowyphoto.com. Courtesy Betty Tatham; (bcl) Johnny Johnson/Animals Animals; (bc) Art Wolfe/Photo Researchers; bcr) Courtesy Helen K. Davie. 112-113: (bkgd) Digital Vision/Getty Images. 114: Royalty-Free/CORBIS;